ANGLING FOR WORDS

Teacher's Line

Dorothy B. Montgomery

**the teacher's guide
for language training**

Academic Therapy Publications
Novato, California

Academic Therapy Publications
20 Commercial Boulevard
Novato, California 94949-6191

International Standard Book Number: 0-87879-105-1

9 8 7 6 5 4 3 2 1 0
0 9 8 7 6 5 4 3 2 1

INTRODUCTION

The Teacher's Challenge

Within the public schools, increasing numbers of students with various learning disabilities are being recognized, diagnosed, and referred to special teachers for remediation. The special education teacher is then faced with the task of selecting and employing the best methods and materials to facilitate learning and will be held directly accountable for pupil progress.

Many of the referred students are of 4th to 12th grade placement because the academic demands at those levels screen student abilities graphically. These students often have average or above-average intelligence but display serious reading and spelling disabilities in spite of good classroom instruction. Referral information at these age levels often does not name a specific sensory deficit (visual, auditory, or motor), and one may not be identifiable. Educational plans from diagnosticians may suggest an approach or method of teaching, but it often remains for the teacher to select the means of instruction as well as material to accomplish the remediation. Only those who have been faced with meeting the needs of these students, often in educational structures far from ideal, know how difficult this can be in its execution.

The Need for Structure

Training for teachers of students with learning disabilities usually stresses the need for careful structuring of student environment, tasks, and learning materials in order to expedite learning. The student with learning disabilities which are clearly evidenced by his performance in the areas of reading, writing, and spelling and who has been unable to learn by traditional methods, needs special methods and materials structured for his difficulties.

Developmental materials designed for students without disability naturally are not so structured, and few materials have been developed for these older students which are both effective and practical.

The Gillingham Method

The Gillingham Method was developed by Anna Gillingham in the 1940's under direction of Samuel Orton, a neuro-psychiatrist specializing in reading disabilities. It was designed as a program of complete language training for students who were medically diagnosed as having a specific disability in reading, spelling, and writing. This problem has been termed specific or developmental dyslexia or specific language disability (SLD). These bright students were unable to learn by the usual predominately visual teaching methods. The Gillingham Method is based on the premise that poor skill in the visual area must be strengthened by support from the auditory, kinesthetic, and motor areas. It places central emphasis on a phonetic approach and logical, sequential structure. The names, sounds, and forms of the letters are the starting point, and enough practice is given to produce automatic response.

Emerald Dechant describes the Gillingham Method in educational terms as:

> . . . a multisensory approach emphasizing the linguistic and graphic regularities of English words. It is termed as alpha-phonetic method . . . It is a combination method, using the auditory, visual, and kinesthetic sense avenues . . . It is a synthetic phonics system rather than an analytical phonics approach . . .
>
> Using the multisensory approach, the Gillingham Method introduces the linguistic and graphically regular words first. Only gradually is the pupil introduced to exceptions.[1]

Gillingham language training as described in *Remedial Training for Children with Specific Disability in Reading, Spelling and Penmanship* by Anna Gillingham and Bessie W. Stillman,[2] has traditionally been utilized by language therapists trained for several years by other Gillingham therapists. Such training is naturally difficult to secure and the manual difficult to use effectively without instruction. The method was designed for a one-to-one teaching structure with daily lessons for a minimum of two years. It aims at providing a level of language ability capable of carrying the student trained by it through college. Adaptations have been made by Beth Slingerland[3] and by Aylett R. Cox, whose manual *Structures and Techniques, Remedial Language Training*[4] for *Alphabetic Phonics*[5] adapts and modifies the Orton-Gillingham-Childs approach in a more practical form for therapists.

Angling for Words

No material had been produced which unified the basic reading-spelling training of the Gillingham Method and was also designed for extended practice with students above primary level. *Angling for Words* was developed for the Summer Language Training Program at the Hockaday School in Dallas, Texas, by Carolyn Bowen and other therapists certified in the Orton-Gillingham-Childs method. It serves as the skeleton material for the language training provided by these experienced therapists. It was structured to guide acquisition of background knowledge about the phonetic and linguistic principles contained in the "codes" in the English language, stressing its regularities. It aims to give a manual skills level on which the student may call when his visual memory or perceptual organization fails him on the automatic level of reading, writing, or spelling. The interrelationship of spelling and reading becomes clearer by use of the Workbook exercises at appropriate points.

Because of the structure and sequence in *Angling for Words*, it can also be used as a tool merely to develop the coding skills, especially decoding in reading. This is particularly meaningful to dedicated teachers without available training in language therapy. Working sequentially through the presentation order in *Angling* at a pace determined by the severity of his disability, a student can experience continued success in word attack, and the teacher is assured that perceptual discrimination and memory weaknesses can be identified and remediated.

Since *Angling for Words* has been used successfully in training with small groups, it adapts itself easily to the needs of the special education teacher and to the increasingly popular resource room structure. In a practical and economical format, it focuses on the basic skill deficiency of so many of the language-disabled students, the decoding and encoding process. These students are unable adequately to decode written letters into the oral word represented or encode an oral word into the letters that spell it in writing. This teacher's manual, written by a Gillingham therapist, using it in the resource room structure of the public school, attempts to supply the minimum background necessary for a special education or trained reading teacher to use *Angling* effectively on the Skills Level. Sections requiring more background skills on the part of the student or the teacher are so marked. A student with combined severe auditory, visual, and motor disabilities will probably need to be taught individually and with the more elaborated procedures outlined in *Structures and Techniques*[6] mentioned above.

WHAT THE TEACHER
NEEDS TO KNOW

About the Student

The student for whom *Angling for Words* was developed has been labeled by many names, and this is a source of real confusion. The term "dyslexic" is commonly used by those of several disciplines, but it has connotations and meanings varying with the discipline of the user and reader. To avoid misconceptions implied by "dyslexia," this manual uses the term "specific language disability" (SLD) and views it as a category within the larger classifications of language and learning disabilities. It has been described as among the mildest of the disorders in the continuum of learning disabilities, but it can be academically crippling.

The term "learning disability," as it is most commonly used in the literature, refers to children of average or above-average intelligence in whom the neurology of learning has been disrupted, changing the psychology by which they learn. They have a dysfunction in the brain not displayed in gross neurological abnormalities. These children then are *not* the mentally retarded, the slow learner, the deaf or blind, or the emotionally disturbed, all of whom may be more easily recognized. Those with learning disabilities possess the intelligence and the organization and use of senses, but they cannot learn in traditional ways. They are usually found in the regular classroom, frequently trying the patience of the teachers who attempt to help them.

In his academic language performance, the student with specific language disability may display all or any of a pattern of characteristics ranging from mild to extreme degrees. His reading is usually slow, inaccurate, and without rhythm, with substitutions and omissions of words which lead to poor comprehension. In spelling, he can sometimes memorize a word list successfully, but spelling in themes, tests, and letters is poor and often bizarre. His handwriting is usually uneven and shows poor letter formation; it is messy and frequently illegible.

Reversals in the order of letters, words, and numbers are very common in both reading and spelling long after the normal tendency toward reversals disappears at about the age of seven. The SLD student cannot easily retain the mental picture of words and may not recognize a memorized word if it is seen in a different context. His visual memory is often so unreliable that he cannot recall a word in order to spell it even if he can recognize it consistently in reading. Despite perfect hearing he will frequently have problems with faulty sound discrimination; his auditory memory for sounds or words is poor, and his auditory attention span short.[7]

With these difficulties handicapping him, it is natural that the student with specific language disability does poorly in the regular classroom. Teachers tend to describe such students as immature, lazy, careless, or inattentive. The hyperactivity, clumsiness, and short attention span seen in children with learning disabilities are especially noticeable in the SLD group. Because they have trouble following directions, lose materials, and cannot copy accurately, their homework is usually of poor quality. They rarely volunteer in class although they can often perform well orally.

The problem of not being able to keep up with his classmates will frequently frustrate the student with specific language disability to distract attention from his inadequacies by showing off, talking constantly, and using aggressive behavior. Or he may withdraw and be silent and shy to avoid attention, suffer chronic anxiety, or succumb to defeatism. He usually has no self-confidence and considers himself stupid; he suffers feelings of discouragement and is often defensive about his shortcomings while resentful of the success of others.

The student with such language disability is usually a male, the common ratio of incidence cited being three or four males to every female, with some sources citing as high as fifteen to one. Estimates on the incidence of specific language disability also vary widely, the variance due primarily to difficulties in diagnosis and research studies. Medical writers tend to estimate disability of a crippling degree in 6 to 10 percent, with an additional 10 percent somewhat affected.

About Language

The term "language disability" indicates difficulties beyond those labeled "reading disability," and it is important for the teacher of such students to have a broad view of language. Teacher education often includes course work in the language arts, and some background knowledge is assumed. A brief review of the ways language development and language disabilities may be viewed might indicate the scope of language training.

Language is a broader phenomenon than just uttering words. It is a complicated system of symbols and, according to Helmer Myklebust, develops first as inner language, then as receptive, and last as expressive language. In developing inner language, meaningfulness and experience must come before the symbols of words. In receptive language, the child learns to understand spoken words, and the aphasias are failures at this level. Mild involvements at this level may not be identified until the child meets the difficult vocabulary of the classroom. Children with problems at the expressive level cannot express themselves adequately. Many children with language disability cannot retrieve an exact word from their memories and will use substitutions. Others cannot learn how to put words together adequately or use the correct muscle patterns for speaking.

Beyond this level on the continuum are the symbol systems deriving from speech, reading, and writing. Education in the language arts focuses progressively on listening and oral expression, then reading and writing. Disabilities can occur anywhere along the continuum of understanding, speaking, reading, and writing, and usually will impair the functioning on the levels above. It is at the level of reading that a large number of children break down in specific language disability and cannot interpret the symbols.[8]

Another way of viewing the continuum of language is its development from the concrete to the abstract. Alfred Korzybski uses an Abstraction Ladder to illustrate the levels of abstraction in words. A child first learns the specific name of a particular cow, Bessie, and then progresses to the category of cow. Continuing up the ladder, the cow is livestock, then a farm asset, an asset, and finally wealth[9]. A child with a language disability frequently cannot categorize on the higher, more abstract levels and remains concrete in his understanding of meanings at the level of cow or livestock.

Myklebust outlines still another Hierarchy of Experience involving language. The child progresses from sensation to perception, the level where so many of the learning disabilities occur. Here are found the visual or auditory discrimination problems. Imagery, at the level above perception, involves the memory processes, and additional difficulties can occur. Beyond imagery is symbolization, and it is at this level that so many children fail. They therefore cannot adequately interpret the printed word, write, or calculate. The fifth level in this hierarchy is conceptualization, in which the child classifies or categorizes according to common elements.[10]

About Written Symbols

A brief look at the written symbols involved in reading and writing may help clarify for the teacher some of the difficulties certain children have with them. Anthropological evidence would indicate that man by 10,000 years ago must have been able to speak rapidly and efficiently. Writing probably began 5,000 years ago and was then in the form of pictures actually representing the objects and activities pictured. The writing always was related to the meaning of the word, not its sound. More complicated picture writing followed, which included more abstract ideas, and persons viewing the pictures could infer meanings in their own terms. This level of writing is termed pictographic and the symbols often called hieroglyphs.[11]

The Phoenicians, for greater efficiency, began using symbols to represent the individual sounds of speech in syllables instead of whole words. The Greeks simplified the letter signs and added vowels, thus compiling the alphabet. Originally, each symbol stood for one sound, and this one-to-one level order of symbolization was not too difficult to learn.

The spoken form of any language changes with use, and the written form cannot change as rapidly. The invention of printing and the need to be able to read print stabilized the written forms in spelling, while the pronunciations continued to change. To complicate things further, the English language reflects words borrowed from many other languages, and many of the spellings of those languages are retained. Although English is basically a phonetic language, these additions cause many irregularities. Nevertheless, a complete understanding of the basic patterns of letters and structures inherent in the English language renders much of English "regular."

Written language is a substitution for the auditory symbols of oral language and is therefore two steps away from the object being symbolized. For the child with difficulties on the symbolization level, the disabilities may soon become evident; for the primary task of the school is to teach the written form of language. Reading of the written form is learned first because it involves recognition and interpretation of what someone else wrote, and this is easier than producing one's own thoughts in writing.[12] Spelling is on a higher level of language skill because its written form requires the simultaneous ability to revisualize and reauditorize letters and then to put them down motorically. It requires discrimination, memory, sequence, analysis, and synthesis; consequently, most children with learning disabilities display deficits in spelling.[13]

About Phonics and Linguistics

Charles Fries, in *Linguistics and Learning*, uses the term "phonics" to represent the teaching practices aimed at developing the ability to sound out words in beginning reading, matching the individual alphabet letters with specific sounds of English pronunciation. "Phonetics," on the other hand, is concerned with describing the sounds of language, their differences, and the ways the differences are pronounced. It is not concerned with the process of reading or how the sounds are conventionally spelled.[14]

The most popular method of teaching beginning reading for some years has been an analytic method concentrating on the whole word as perceived as a configuration. Frequently an analytical phonics method is also applied, and the whole word which has been learned is then broken down into its basic sound elements.[15] Linguists sometimes criticize phonics as it is taught in the schools, claiming that it may not be based on linguistically sound information. Example: "When two vowels go walking, the first one does the talking."

Children with specific language disability frequently cannot learn to read adequately by the whole word method because of their difficulties in perceiving the word as a whole or in retaining its visual image. The phonic method utilized in *Angling for Words* is a synthetic phonic method which starts with the letters of the alphabet and the phonetic sounds of these letters and letter patterns and blends these into words. Knowledge of the functioning of structural units like syllables and suffixes are also of prime importance in this approach. Added to this, from the study of linguistics, is the emphasis on automatic response to the features of contrasting spelling patterns to identify the word patterns they represent. The position of a letter in a word or syllable, its sequence with adjacent letters, and accent are clues to its pronunciation. For example: an a before a consonant is read with a short sound, am; in an open accented syllable, it has the long sound, bacon; in a vowel-consonant-silent e letter pattern, it is pronounced with the long sound, cake; in an open, unaccented syllable, it has an obscure sound, along; before an r its sound may be altered in a manner that depends on accent and what letter follows the r: star, card, dollar, care, charity, carry. Combinations of consonants or vowel letters into digraphs are symbols for specific sounds. To the child who cannot remember the mental picture of a word and has no knowledge of any system of language structure, such information may be his only means to unlock the mystery of printed symbols.

In describing the alphabetic code of written language representing oral speech, Aylett Cox points out the following: The 26 letters of the alphabet are used to represent at least 44 basic sounds. Fifteen letters represent only one sound, in whatever position they are used (b, d, f, h, j, k, l, m, p, q, r, t, v, w, and z); their sounds can usually be determined by removing the vowel sound from the oral pronunciation of their letter names. Of the other 11 single letters, five have two sounds each, (g, n, s, x, y). Of the remaining six, c, e, and i represent at least two sounds, and only a, o, u, and y regularly have more than two.[16]

The use of spelling principles as clues to accurate reading involves the knowledge of what is the "regular" or usual performance of sounds and letters in given situations. The spelling of the sound can be considered regular in initial, medial, or final position in a syllable or word. The "regular" spelling is reliable in most instances and should be used in spelling unfamiliar words. The information deeming a phonogram "regular" used in *Angling for Words* is based on *Phoneme-Grapheme Correspondence as Cues to Spelling Improvement*,[17] directed by Paul

9

Hanna and published by the U.S. Department of Health, Education, and Welfare, the Gillingham manual, and presentations by Aylett R. Cox in *Situation Reading*[18] and *Situation Spelling*.[19]

Some information from phonetics can be helpful to the teacher in understanding the auditory confusions evidenced by some students. Most of the consonant sounds have partners; that is, both of the pair of sounds are produced with the lips, tongue, mouth, and throat in identical position. In production of one of the pair, the vocal chords in the larynx vibrate, and the sound is called "voiced"; in the other, the chords do not vibrate and it is termed "unvoiced". These pairs include: (b)-(p); (d)-(t); (g)-(k); (v)-(f); (z)-(s); (j)-(ch); (zh)-(sh); (gz)-(ks). This pairing explains the two pronunciations for s, x, and -sion.[20] Normal speech production usually takes care of the choice between the pairs, for instance: in pronouncing the -ed suffix, it is sailed (d), jumped (t), and rented, landed (ĕd), depending upon the letter sound preceding the ed. Students with common (f)-(v) confusion will often display it in speech and in writing. The (b)-(p) causes some auditory confusion and has the added difficulty of encouraging graphic form reversals, b - p.

About Manual and Automatic Levels of Reading

In learning to read, the manual level of dealing with written symbols must first be perfected. In a phonetic language, the manual level in reading is reacting to the visual stimulus of a word, speaking it, and comprehending the idea contained in it. In spelling, the idea comes first, then the spoken word, then the written symbol for the spoken sound. Most competent readers, as they acquire the ability to use reading and writing with automaticity, are unconscious that they are even using visual symbols for objects and ideas. Scanning the printed line is mechanical as the stimuli are sent to the brain, which integrates them into a pattern which can be recognized and compared with stored memories. The spoken word is not needed and meaning comes directly from the written word as the automatic level is achieved. In spelling on the automatic level, the idea leads directly to the written word, by-passing the spoken word. The aim is for the student to operate on the automatic level virtually all of the time in both reading and writing.[21]

The difficulty faced by many students with specific language disability is in achieving even the lowest manual level of decoding and encoding. The words he must learn to decode are frequently already meaningful in the student's oral vocabulary, and once the basic manual skill is developed, he can progress in the other vital reading skills. To interpret the language he is learning to decode requires real knowledge of the structure of language on the part of the teacher.

Emerald V. Dechant in *Improving the Teaching of Reading*, discussing reading instruction, says of word recognition through phonics instruction:

> It is the process of lawfully decoding the unknown written word through the application of one's knowledge of grapheme-phoneme correspondences. It is not enough to know that the pupil needs to learn a coding system. The teacher needs to be able to organize his presentation of words in beginning reading in such a way that children can break the code rather than have to learn each word independently . . . Pupils need to learn how words are structured and how the arrangement of letters in a word controls the way the letters function.[22]

Even more meaningful is this admonition in the consideration of the needs of the SLD student. *Angling for Words* and this manual are dedicated to meeting the needs of these students and their teachers.

About the Structuring of English

In learning to deal with written symbols in language, the student who has difficulties in sequencing and orderliness, in addition to problems in perception or memory, needs the material he is to learn already structured for him. This, of course, is the primary function of *Angling for Words*.

Valuable background for the teacher's full understanding of the concept of structure in language is found in "The Structure of English: The Language To Be Learned," by Margaret B. Rawson.[23] She describes the development of language in the preschool child as he learns the grammar, word order, and word form of the language spoken around him. She states:

> Normally, no matter what his background, by six he is ready to learn to read anything he can understand when he hears it from outside his head, or from within, in his thinking. He has mastered *one* code – the system of translating into ideas the sounds-in-sequence which you and I know as words.[24]

The second code to be learned, therefore, transforms speech into visible print in space-patterns that are matched, or approximately matched, to the sound patterns of speech. The letter forms of the alphabet may be written in variant forms of print and handwriting, in capital or lower-case letters; they are space-oriented, as b-d-p-q, and combine to form graphemes which represent the audible phonemes. This second code permits encoding speech into writing and, in reading, decoding writing into speech which may or may not actually involve the vocal chords.[25]

The English alphabet contains only 26 symbols, with at least 24 consonants and 14 or more vowel sounds making up the phonemes or basic sound units. Mastering the English code involves, necessarily, the memorization of the 26 letter forms. Even learning the additional letter-sound patterns and the principles of coding leaves us with a much easier task than learning a large number of sight words. If the reader knows enough about the spelling conventions in English, the system is over 85 percent predictable. Even the "non-phonetic" words usually have some predictable phonemes which will permit a reasonable guess in reading.[26]

The Orton-Gillingham-Childs approach is to firmly establish the phoneme-grapheme correspondences by multisensory practice until they become automatic. The unfolding of the code, by which the English language structures the phonemes and graphemes, moves from the simplest combinations to the complex in logical sequence. Attention is focused on the position of letters in a syllable or word and on understanding this position as a clue to pronunciation and spelling. Emphasis on base words to which prefixes and suffixes are added helps develop perception of units larger than individual letters and facilitates the grasp of meaning.

The order of presentation of phonograms for reading in *Angling for Words* begins with short vowels in closed monosyllables with unequivocal consonants and moves to include consonant blends, doubled consonants, and words of several closed syllables. At this level phonetic spelling can correlate with the reading and reinforce the mastery of this large group of English words. Long vowels are introduced in open syllables accented at the end of words and in vowel-consonant-*e* patterns. Consonant digraphs and the vowel-*r* situation follow for reading, but spelling is no longer completely regular and requires consideration of the position of sounds. The presentation of vowel-consonant-vowel patterns builds on previous learning of the code for reading and focuses on the influence of syllable division and accent on vowel sound. Vowel digraphs and diphthongs are then introduced and mastered, greatly increasing the words decodable for reading. Finally, other alternatives of pronunciation are presented in groups, along with silent letters, letter combinations and suffixes, and more complicated patterns of syllable division. The emphasis is always upon the regularity of the patterns in the code, and the student is never presented a phonogram to read which has not been studied.

About Multisensory Teaching

The sensory modalities involved in difficulties with perception are, of course, the visual, auditory, kinesthetic, and tactile systems. Lucius Waites, a pediatric neurologist specializing in specific language disability, points out that perceptual difficulties are among the most common neuropsychological problems found in children and that difficulties in perception and cognition in the sensory systems result in language disability. Visual imperception in the form of specific language disability seems to be the most common of the language disabilities, usually evidenced in problems in reading, writing, and spelling. Waites adds:

> Other forms of imperception usually accompany visual imperception, but not invariably. The most common of the complications is visual-motor incoordination . . . Kinesthetic imperception is the least commonly recognized of the perceptual difficulties and is difficult to delineate in pure form. However, it frequently complicates the other types . . . Clinical signs that accompany kinesthetic imperception are poor writing, incoordination, clumsiness, spatial confusion, and inability to copy patterns.[27]

At the time of the development of the Gillingham Method, its emphasis on multisensory training was unique. Devised under the guidance of a neurologist, its basic tenet was that through the consistent and simultaneous use of all the sensory avenues, the child's weaker perceptions are strengthened by the reaction of the stronger ones. The child with poor visual memory for letter-arrangement in words, seen in specific language disability, is thus trained to compensate with his stronger auditory perception, and a phonetic approach is logical. Gillingham holds that there must be structured daily drills on concepts taught one at a time, and presented through all avenues of perception in the same sequential steps. The student therefore learns by seeing the letter, saying and hearing its name and sound, feeling its shape tactilely, and feeling it kinesthetically as he writes it with his large muscles. Patterns for new learning are established, regardless of which of the perceptions are weak. Dr. Waites expresses the opinion accepted by many medical men in this field that a "multisensory approach to training has proved successful for such children and must be basic whether used at the primary level or in the course of later retraining."[28]

WHAT THE TEACHER
WANTS TO KNOW

What Teaching Structure Makes the Use of *Angling for Words* Most Effective?

1. Teacher's full attention and interaction.
2. Limited distractions in surroundings.
3. Student group with less than five students.
4. Grouping by approximate degree of severity of language disability.
5. Individualized lessons.

What Materials Are Needed to Use *Angling for Words* as a Program?

1. A classroom copy of the *Angling Study Book* for the teacher and each student's use.
2. One classroom copy of the *Angling Workbook* for each student's use for training on the Skills Level. On the Advanced Level, each student would need his own consumable workbook.
3. One manual, *The Teacher's Line*.
4. One set of *Angling Phono-Cards* for each group of lesson preparation.
5. Student notebooks or folders.
6. Blackboard.

For Which Students Is *Angling for Words* Designed or Useful?

1. Students diagnosed as having specific or developmental dyslexia or SLD (specific language disability).

2. Students with diagnosed learning disability who have average or above-average intelligence, no deficits in sight or hearing acuity, but with below-grade-level performance in word attack, reading, and spelling.

3. Students with diagnosed problems in visual memory and/or discrimination needing a structured phonetic reading approach and multisensory teaching.*

4. Students who have perhaps outgrown earlier perceptual problems but need a highly structured form of training to catch up with their peers in reading and spelling.

5. As a resource tool, *Angling for Words* is useful with various types of students as drill material in word attack or specific phoneme weaknesses.

What Testing Results Might Indicate the Use of *Angling*?

Results of several types of tests should combine to suggest use. Information which is possibly already in student file or referral:

1. Intelligence test score – Student scores of 90 or above are a prerequisite for complete understanding of *Angling* as a language training program and the reasoning principles inherent in the spelling training. It may be used with discretion for reading instruction with students of lower ability.

2. *Wide Range Achievement Test-3* (WRAT-3) – The reading and spelling tests are checks of sight recognition, decoding, and encoding. Spelling test may reveal reversals, omissions, or bizarre combinations of letters. Grade equivalent scores are helpful in indicating severity of the disability.

3. Other standardized achievement tests – Extremely low scores on vocabulary tests read silently should contrast with higher scores on an oral test. Low grade-level scores on spelling tests requiring recognition of incorrect spellings are often indicative of SLD.

4. *Illinois Test of Psycholinguistic Abilities* (ITPA) – Low scores on subtests for visual abilities may indicate SLD tendencies.

5. Oral reading test results (as in Gray Oral) – Students often make multiple errors on gross mispronunciations, substitutions, omissions, and inversions indicating word attack difficulties.

---

* Experience has shown that some disabilities in auditory and motor function frequently become evident with careful screening of a student with an obvious visual disability. The term "auditory learner" should be interpreted as naming his strongest pathway and not indicating that he is without any auditory weaknesses.

Screening Tests

1. *Individual Learning Disabilities Classroom Screening Instrument* (ILDCSI)[29] – Adolescent Level, Grades 4-12. High percentile scores on Visual Disabilities with probable involvement indicated on Auditory, Motor, and Integrational scores.

2. *Screening Tests for Identifying Children with Specific Language Disabilities*[30] designed for individual or group testing, grades 1-2, 3-4, 5-6. Subtests evaluate various visual, auditory, and motor integrations.

3. *Specific Language Disability Test*[31] is not normed; performance indicates weaknesses in specific integrations.

Informal Tests for Specific Information on Difficulties:

1. *Dolch Basic Sight Vocabulary* – Excessive errors can indicate severity of visual memory difficulties.

2. Graded word lists for grade level and types of problems:
   a. Iota Word List[32]
   b. The Graded Word List[33]
   c. Informal Word Recognition Inventory[34]
   d. Monroe Spelling List[35]

3. *Angling* Phonetic Skills Survey (in Appendix of this manual).

4. Teacher checks:
   a. Alphabet – The ability to recite it, write it; write while timed (in cursive); read vertical lists of single letters in random order rapidly.
   b. Spelling of common irregular words: to, of, would, these, they, been, some, know, write, should, once, could, want, who, said, only, Mrs., many.
   c. Correct cursive letter forms (capital and small, separate and connected.)

WHAT THE TEACHER SHOULD KNOW

About the Materials for *Angling for Words:*

The Study Book

1. Read the first three pages of the book carefully, noting explanations of abbreviations, underlining, and definitions used in the book.

2. Note especially the explanation of the fish symbol for Workbook exercises; if the fish is on right of page, use exercise after page, if on left, use before the text page.

3. Nonsense words are always listed below asterisks (***).

4. Primary type with serifs and wide spacing are used for visual discrimination.

5. The phonetic symbols used in *Angling* are simple and easily learned.

6. In accordance with linguistic principles, there are no pictures in the Study Book to detract from the decoding being learned.

7. The use of minimal contrasting pairs for drill (pit-pat; mop-mope) is also a principle from linguistics and develops auditory and visual discrimination.

8. The division of the Study Book into seven logical levels for sequence and concepts provides good structure for objectives and evaluations as well as promoting feelings of accomplishment for the student.

9. The sequence in phonogram introduction in the Study Book is completely structured, and no letter or sound is ever used before it has been presented. Thus the student can succeed with the familiar.

10. A time lapse in presentation is used with letters easily confused, (p-b, d-b) to strengthen discrimination and secure knowledge of letter shapes.

11. Learned (irregular) words are kept to an absolute minimum in the reading sentences to stress the concept of regularity. The irregular words used are listed above the sentence sections for the teacher's easy use.

19

The Workbook

1. Although the numbering of the exercise pages within the fish symbols in the Study Book may appear illogical, the Table of Contents of the Workbook will reveal the logical grouping of concepts. Do not work straight through the pages in the Workbook!

2. The key words and sound pictures for the reading and spelling *Phono-Cards* are listed on pages 1-4.

3. Exercises of spelling from sound pictures strengthen the concept of symbols representing sounds and also test understanding of spelling rules and conventions.

4. The section of exercises on syllable division visually strengthens concepts of the relationship of syllable division to pronunciation and spelling.

5. Sheets are punched for notebooks and may be removed for student use in advanced spelling training.

The Teacher's Line

1. Three levels of use for *Angling* are indicated in this manual:
   a. Skills Level – regular phonetic decoding training, strengthened by daily drills with cards. All material not marked TT or AA is for Skills Level training and can be used by the less-able student.
   b. Thought Level – marked TT; materials requiring some learning of principles or some reasoning. Teacher can individualize with this level according to need.
   c. Advanced Level – marked AA; coding principles, especially in spelling, which require more abstract thinking from the student and greater background knowledge on the part of the teacher. This material may not be necessary or "worth the effort" for many students. There are "traps" in the language structure that a teacher could fall into.

2. Descriptions of basic techniques and teacher tips to be used throughout the training are presented before *The Teacher's Line* section of the manual. Techniques are variations of Orton-Gillingham-Childs methods adapted for the *Angling* program through classroom experience.

3. *The Teacher's Line* section contains instructions and background for pages, keys to Workbook exercises, and sample spelling drills provided in running commentary form under the page numbers of the Study Book. Pace is always determined by the needs of the individual students.

4. Sample behavioral objectives for each of the levels in *Angling* are included at the beginning of the level.

5. The Appendix contains sample sheets teacher may copy.

   a. *Angling* Phonetic Skills Survey and instructions.

   b. Sample daily lesson plan form.

   c. Sample tests for each level which may be used as pre- and/or post-tests.

   d. Sample chart to graph reading phonograms to provide motivation.

Phono-Cards

1. *Angling Phono-Cards* are designed to implement a language training program using *Angling for Words*. They follow the order of presentation, techniques, and concepts of the *Angling* Study Book and Workbook and the instructions in *The Teacher's Line*. Other published cards for the Orton-Gillingham-Childs approach can be adapted to the *Angling* program.

2. Key words on the reading *Phono-Cards* were selected to demonstrate the pure phonetic pronunciation (in initial position when possible) and to represent objects and experiences common to most students. Other key words may be substituted if the teacher chooses.

3. The vowel and consonant reading cards are of different colors to strengthen the recognition of the difference but are mixed together in use. These cards are numbered on the back as a set to indicate the order of introduction for reading followed in *Angling for Words*; introduced cards are shuffled daily to change the order of presentation.

4. Technique 2 in the next section of *The Teacher's Line* describes the daily use of the reading *Phono-Cards*.

5. The spelling *Phono-Cards* are of a different color and are numbered in the order of presentation of the first response given in *Angling*. Additional responses are learned and added at the point indicated in *The Teacher's Line*.

6. The teacher follows Technique 2 in the use of the cards, giving the sound in parenthesis at the top of the card for the student to respond by repeating the sound and naming the letter spelling and any conditions which have been learned as they are listed on the card. The key words in slashes are only used to aid the teacher in interpreting the phonetic picture or for prompting a student response.

Student Notebooks

1. On the Advanced level of training it is important for each student to have his own copy of the Workbook so that exercise sheets may be pulled out and placed in notebook upon completion. Notebooks for this level are described in *Angling*. This structure promotes visual retention of concepts and orderliness.

2. On the Skills Level and Thought Level (TT), it is recommended that the student keep a simple notebook, with sections or pages to include:
    a. Chart of phonograms introduced for reading to show progress.
    b. List of regular spellings introduced, listed as they are covered, in the form used on Workbook pages 3-4. (This is usually too difficult to chart or graph.)
    c. Spelling and syllable division rules copied from Workbook or teacher presentation. (TT)
    d. Spelling and syllable division drills done in class on notebook paper.
    e. List of irregular words learned for reading by Technique 4.
    f. List of irregular words learned for spelling by Technique 5.

About Techniques to Use with *Angling*

Technique 1

For the teacher's first introduction of a letter for reading:
    1. Show letter on reading card (V)* – name it (A).
    2. Say key word and sound distinctly (A).
    3. Students repeat the name, key word, and sound (A).
    4. Write the letter, oversize and in cursive, on blackboard or large paper, emphasizing the downstrokes in the cursive letter form.
    5. Students copy its form by writing it large in air, using large arm muscles (V-K).
    6. Students then copy the letter (V) (K), large on blackboard or paper, while naming it (A). If performance is weak, have them also write it (K) in air with eyes closed, or trace on table top, sandpaper, etc. (T).
    7. Name letter (A) – students give key word and sound (A).
    8. Dictate sound (A) – students give letter spelling (A) while writing it (K) or tracing (T).

 * Capital letter denotes the sensory modality stimulated in the student: V-visual; A-auditory; K-kinesthetic; T-tactile.

Technique 2

Use of reading cards for daily drill:
    1. Shuffle stack of the reading *Phono-Cards* already introduced by Technique 1.
    2. Hold as a deck, with the letter facing students. (V)

* Capital letter denotes the sensory modality stimulated in the student: V-visual; A-auditory; K-kinesthetic; T-tactile.

   3. Students respond to sight of card by giving the memorized key word and sound (V-A) listed on the back. When two responses are learned to a letter, they are given in the order listed.
   4. Turn card down and continue through cards at a rapid pace.

Note: The name of the letter is not given as a response at this age level unless the student displays weakness in letter names.

Use of spelling cards for daily drill:

   1. Shuffle and hold the spelling *Phono-Cards* for those sounds which have been introduced as regular for spelling.
   2. Cards are not shown to students in this drill; printed side faces teacher.
   3. Give sound indicated by sound picture on top card (A) – students respond by repeating the sound, naming the letter or letters learned for spelling it (A) and any conditions for spelling. The student writes it in large cursive in air or on blackboard (K), tabletop (T), or paper (K), whichever is most effective for the student's learning patterns. (This *writing* of the sound may gradually be omitted as a *daily* response as spelling dictation increases and student displays firm knowledge.)

Technique 3

Spelling dictation:

   1. Pronounce the word, emphasizing consonant and vowel sounds clearly. (A)
   2. Student repeats word, pronouncing it in syllables. Base word should be pronounced, then suffix. (A)
   3. Student writes the word in cursive (K), naming the letters as he writes (A). In student groups this naming can be done subvocally.
   4. Student reads the written word aloud, exactly as he wrote it, as a proofreading check. (V-A)
   5. Check word, marking which words have mistakes. Student should discover the specific error and correct it, preferably at the next lesson.

Note: Spelling the whole word orally before writing it is helpful to many students and can easily be done in an individual teaching situation. In a group, one student might spell the word orally before the group writes.

Dictation of phrases or sentences on Skills Level:

1. Read aloud the complete phrase or sentence.
2. Repeat by dictating logical short units one at a time, with student repeating and spelling each unit by the procedure outlined above.
3. Length of phrase or sentence can be individualized and used as training in auditory memory.

Technique 4

Irregular words are kept to a minimum in *Angling*, but the following procedure can be used to teach irregular words for reading:

1. Print the word on an index card. Print the sound picture on the back of the card.
2. Pronounce the word carefully by syllables for the student as he looks at card (V-A). He repeats (V-A).
3. Discuss irregularities in the word and identify irregular letters in the word (these may be underlined). (V)
4. Student copies the word (V-K), writing in oversize cursive, naming each letter aloud as he writes (V-A).
5. Student checks his word with model (V) and reads it aloud (A).
6. Additional tactile reinforcement may be given by tracing letters on paper or rough surface (T).
7. Choice of learned words should be individualized, and each student should have his own card pack to drill from.

Technique 5

Spelling irregular words:

1. Word should have been learned for reading by Technique 4.
2. Discuss elements in the word irregular for *spelling* (V-A).
3. Write the word in cursive, pronouncing it in syllables and naming the letters. (V-A)
4. Student traces the letters (V-T), naming the letters (A).
5. Student reads word and copies, naming letters as he writes (V-A-K). Copy several times.
6. For individual learning style, student may write word in air, using whole arm (K) and saying each letter as he writes (A).
7. Without model, student writes the word (K), saying each letter as he writes (A). He reads what he wrote (A).

8. Reinforce steps if necessary by repeating the steps using the student's strongest modality.

9. Learned words should be reviewed frequently in spelling dictations.

Tips for Teaching with *Angling*

General Teaching Techniques

1. Nothing motivates like success, and the structure of *Angling* is designed to promote success.

2. If at all possible, arrange for student's school reading assignments to be read to him or taped while he is learning to succeed in decoding. This is particularly important when the habit of wild guessing must be broken.

3. These students respond well to the set routine of the ordered lesson plan, but pace must stay brisk and motivating. Shift activities rapidly to hold attention. Vary the manner of the spelling drills (blackboard, magic slates, writing in air or on table). Find ways for hyperactive students to move around.

4. Use discovery techniques for concepts, have races writing the alphabet, let students drill each other in pairs with the reading and spelling decks when progress allows (only occasionally though!). Interject interesting background information on backgrounds of particular words in the text.

5. Auditory discrimination practice is a good pace-breaker. Say a word and student responds with the vowel spelling; practice counting syllables in various manners; practice shifting accent in syllables or different words in a sentence for meaning.

Using the Study Book

1. The number of regular and/or nonsense words read aloud in daily practice depends on the severity of the disability, size of the group, and individual differences. The amount of each page covered also varies with these.

2. For a good pace with a group of four students, each in turn might read four or five words (vertically).

3. Allow students with problems in keeping the pace on the page to use finger or card under words, or to block out other parts of the page.

4. Note that in columns with contrasting pairs or groups, such as *dell-dill* on page 15 or digraph groups, such as on page 192, the student reads across the group, not vertically in columns.

Nonsense Words

1. Nonsense words *could* be real words if we chose to give them a meaning. They follow all the rules for pronunciation and spelling of real words.
2. Nonsense words are the only way to really check phonetic mastery in early short words when students are older or have a fair sight vocabulary. They are not needed or provided as much on higher levels.
3. Note carefully the reactions of individual students to reading nonsense words. Those with severe disabilities are often disturbed by them and should concentrate on the real words they do not know how to read.
4. Students with less severe disabilities may express dislike of nonsense words because of fear of failure. Many like to treat them as a game or challenge.

Using the Phono-Cards

1. Practice all key words and sounds before introducing them to students. Practice saying them distinctly and without any "uh" after consonants.
2. Learn to read sound pictures on spelling cards rapidly; pace in drill should be as brisk as possible to promote automatic response.
3. For convenience, put rubberbands around spelling pack and the reading pack which have been introduced for drill. A pencil mark can mark which responses students have covered.
4. After a large number of phonograms are introduced, occasionally time drill packs and work for shorter times.

Spelling

1. Check teacher-made spelling lists carefully to ensure that all phonograms included have been covered and that only words regular for *spelling* are included (for example: ai, ea, igh, oa are regular for reading but not spelling). Note how sample lists cover and check varied structures through choice of words.
2. Do not stress handwriting form in spelling dictation because the degree of integration demanded by spelling demands full attention to the spelling
3. Proofreading what he has actually written is essential for SLD students; this gives practice in reading what is actually there and strengthens analytical approach. Keep emphasizing proofreading, despite student complaints, until habit is ingrained.

Handwriting

1. Oversized writing is stressed for kinesthetic training of large muscles.
2. With severe handwriting problems, writing on notebook paper for spelling or practice should be at least two lines high with a line skipped between words.

Setting the Stage with the Students

1. It is important to develop the mental set in the students that they are *not* stupid or strange. Language skill can vary like musical ability but can be learned. Many are relieved to learn that such problems with reading and spelling are so common. Famous men like Einstein, Thomas Edison, Woodrow Wilson, and General George Patton had similar difficulties. They overcame, and the *Angling* program will help today's students with similar problems.

2. Many students can become very objective about their particular types of difficulties and learn to joke about them as they become conscious of them.

3. Approach the first letter introductions with a light touch and reassurance that even adults start just this way. Suggest that they can pretend they don't know any letters or sounds as they are introduced this way to be sure that any "holes" in their background knowledge are filled. To make sure that they really know the phonograms, they will be using all their senses – sight, hearing, and touch. Their muscles will need to feel the shapes by writing in air. Then the muscles won't need to think about how to make a letter.

4. Move as fast as possible in the first few days of training to get a working number of letters introduced but be absolutely thorough in early training or retraining may be later necessary.

5. Assure students that *Angling* will never ask the unknown. Stress the 85 percent regularity of English that can be learned.

6. Administering the *Angling* Phonetic Skills Survey (found in the Appendix of this manual) individually will give the teacher indications of the severity of disability in using phonetic skills. It makes an excellent pre- and post-test.

7. Within the first few days, survey student background on the following skills and concepts:
   a. Check knowledge of alphabet (see previous section on testing).
   b. Check cursive letter forms; correct errors in form as that letter is introduced.

c. What is a *vowel*? (Vowel sounds are open and can be continued with air coming out.) Name them. Should include y with a, e, i, o, and u. *Angling* doesn't consider w a vowel.

d. What is a *consonant*? (All other letters besides vowels; air is blocked by teeth, tongue, or lips.)

e. What is a *syllable*? (A word or part of word said with one push of the voice; it has only one vowel *sound* but may have more vowel letters – sail.)

f. What is a *closed syllable*? (A consonant after the vowel closes it (ham, am); the vowel then has the *short* sound.)

g. What is an *open syllable*? (It ends in a spoken vowel with no consonant closing it. If accented, it has the *long* sound, the sound of its letter name: me. y is as ī.)

h. The term "sound picture" stands for symbols showing how to pronounce letters. A picture has a frame – so these have ( ). Noticed in the dictionary?

8. Instructions in *The Teacher's Line* sections to follow assume a following of the lesson plan order suggested in Appendix. Do not assume to do a page of the Study Book a day, etc., but move according to individual or group ability as you are assured of it.

9. Prepare to be surprised by the things assumed a student could do which this training will reveal he cannot do. Do not assume any real written language mastery by these students until they have proved it.

Important

Read through the explanation in the Study Book at the beginning of Level I and study the "Concepts to Develop." These concepts are expanded in the explanations for the appropriate pages in *The Teacher's Line*, but this summary gives the teacher an excellent overview and frame of reference for Level I.

THE TEACHER'S LINE

Level I (pages 1-57)

Reading and Spelling Evaluation Tests-I in the Appendix can be used for pre- and/or post-tests. They reflect Skills and Thought Level concepts for this section.

Sample Behavioral Objectives for Level I – Skills Level training:

Upon the completion of Level I, for reading:

1. When presented with the 32 reading Phono-Cards introduced in Level I, the student must be able to recall and respond orally with the key word and correct phonetic sound for each card with 100 percent accuracy.

2. When presented with reading cards for the 32 phonograms introduced in Level I, the student must be able to give the letter names on the cards with 100 percent accuracy.

3. When presented with Test I-A list of 20 words containing only phonograms and concepts introduced from pages 4-20 of the *Angling for Words* Study Book, the student will demonstrate his ability to read the list orally with 90 percent accuracy.

4. When presented with Test I-B list of 10 nonsense words containing only phonograms and concepts introduced in pages 4-20 of the *Angling* Study Book, the student will demonstrate his ability to read the list orally with 80 percent accuracy.

5. When presented with Test I-C list of 20 words containing only phonograms and concepts introduced within pages 4-57 of the *Angling* Study Book, the student will demonstrate his ability to read the list orally with 90 percent accuracy.

6. When presented with Test I-D list of 5 nonsense words containing only phonograms and concepts presented within pages 4-57 of the *Angling* Study Book, the student will demonstrate his ability to read the list orally with 80 percent accuracy.

7. When presented with 5 phrases in Test I-E containing only phonograms presented in Level I of *Angling*, the student will demonstrate his ability to read the phrases orally with 100 percent accuracy.

8. When presented with 5 sentences of between 5 and 12 word lengths and containing only phonograms presented in Level I (Test I-F), the student will demonstrate his ability to read the sentences orally with 80 percent accuracy.

TT9. When presented with a list of 5 words and 5 nonsense words, each containing only phonograms presented in Level I and the letter c before a vowel (Test I-G), the student will demonstrate his ability to read the list orally with 80 percent accuracy.

TT10. When presented with a list of 10 words containing only phonograms from Level I and ending in the suffix -ed (Test I-H), the student will demonstrate his ability to read the list orally with 90 percent accuracy.

Upon completion of Level I, for *spelling*:

1. When presented with the oral sound for each of the 27 phonemes covered for spelling in Level I in *Angling for Words*, the student will demonstrate the ability to repeat the sound, name the letter or letters spelling the sound (30 responses), and write the letter or letters named in correct cursive writing form with 80 percent accuracy.

2. Upon dictation of the Test I-1 list of 10 words containing only phonograms regular for spelling covered in pages 4-20 of *Angling* and the ff, ll, ss rule, the student will demonstrate his ability to write the correct spelling of at least 8 words.

3. The student, upon presentation by dictation the Test I-2 list of 8 nonsense words containing only phonograms regular for spelling covered on pages 4-20 of Angling and the ff, ll, ss rule, will demonstrate his ability to write the correct spelling of at least 6 words.

TT4. The student, upon dictation of Test I-3 containing 10 words and 5 nonsense words of phonograms covered in Level I for spelling and the (k) generalization, will demonstrate his ability to write the correct spelling for at least 11 words.

TT5. Upon dictation of Test I-4 with 5 phrases containing only phonograms and generalizations covered in Level I, the student will demonstrate his ability to spell correctly at least 10 of the 14 words in the phrases.

THE TEACHER'S LINE

Level I

Study Book – Page 4

1. Introduce, as fast as they can really be absorbed, i̱ (ĭ), t̲, p̲, n̲, and s̲ (both sounds and key words for s̲) by Technique 1. Be sure the students learn the key words and sounds: i̱ - i̱t (ĭ), t̲ - t̲able (t), p̲ - p̲ig (p), n̲ - n̲est (n), and s̲ - s̲ock (s), n̲ose (z). An s̲ is naturally pronounced (s) after unvoiced consonant sounds and (z) after voiced consonants.

2. Practice blending by arrangement of cards on the table and changing cards. Make sure that a consonant always follows (closes) the i̱.

3. Students read top of page 4 for practice, amount depending on skill; non-sense words at the bottom make good checks. Remind students that you do not pronounce a double consonant but once.

4. The essential concept here is that a vowel (here i̱) in a *closed* syllable (with the vowel followed by one or more consonants) has the short sound. Almost all of Level I is of this pattern.

5. Spelling – Review the 6 sounds learned and their regular spellings by use of the spelling cards and Technique 2: (ĭ) - i̱, (t) - t̲, (p) - p̲, (n) - n̲, (s) - s̲, and (z) - s̲. Do not add any other second spellings until so instructed. Remember that the key word is not given in the spelling response. An s̲ is the regular spelling for the (z) sound except at the beginning of a word, when it is z̲. Do not use words with s̲s̲ for spelling yet.

6. Check student knowledge of capitals at the beginning of sentences and for proper names.

7. Sample spelling dictation:

1. nip	4. tins	Nonsense Words:	
2. sin	5. spit	7. stit	9. tist
3. pits	6. snips	8. nisp	10. ip

It tips. Spin it. Nip sips it.

Page 5

1. The *Phono-Cards* already introduced are reviewed *daily* according to Technique 2, reading cards before reading practice and spelling cards before spelling. See sample lesson plan in Appendix.

2. Add a - apple (ă) and then l - leaf (l) by Technique 1. Both are regular for reading and spelling.

3. Practice in *Angling* after each introduction. Notice that columns of practice words progress in difficulty and length of word from left to right.

4. Go over the concept of *sound pictures* – symbols telling how a letter or letters sound: (ă), (l). The short vowel mark is called a breve. Silent letters are not pictured: inn is (ĭn). Could the students write the sound picture for *spit* (spĭt) or as (ăz)?

5. Include the words I for a for regular reading and spelling. They are *open* syllables and long sounds. Pronounce the word a as (ā) in spelling dictation now, not the unaccented (ə).

6. Add spelling cards (ă) and (l) to the spelling card pack.

7. Spelling dictation:

1. tan	4. pant	7. lips	10. pin in a pan
2. sap	5. snip	8. past	11. in a snap
3. as	6. spat	9. slap	12. at a span

at last; a split; Slap an ant. Tip laps it. Plant it.

Page 6

1. Review expanded card stack using Technique 2. Add d - dog (d). It is regular for reading and spelling. Do not add ed response.

2. Watch for visual and/or writing reversals of d and confusion with p; some students have auditory discrimination problems with (t - d). If necessary, correct with multisensory drill and discrimination practice.

3. Add (d) - d card to spelling stack.

4. Spelling: Nonsense

1. pan	4. last	7. stand	nasp
2. lid	5. slit	8. snap	plit
3. sip	6. asp	9. spins	sland

as Dad did; dip sand; Plan as Sid had. Tilt a pan lid.

5. Emphasize s as a suffix for plural and present verb form. This should be taught as spelling rules if the student is not already familiar with them: The regular plural of a noun is spelled by adding s; third person singular verbs add s. Develop the concept of a suffix added to a base word. (TT)

6. WORKBOOK – page 111 – Students read the completed sentences aloud. KEY:

2. asps; 3. slips, snips, plants; 4. tilts, splints, pins; 5. stilts, spins, lands;

6. pats, naps; 7. pills

Page 7

1. Remember daily review of *Phono-Cards* by Technique 2.

2. Add f - fish (f), regular for reading and spelling. Practice.

3. WORKBOOK – page 5 – Introduce spelling rule on ff, ll, ss. Stress the f, l, or s must directly follow the short vowel. Rule may be learned by chanting, copying, etc. Obvious exceptions in familiar words: us, bus, plus, gas, yes, pal, if, and (z) of s: as, is, was, his, has; and of. Unscrambling exercise
TT   is to reinforce the pattern of a double letter belonging at the end, immediately after the short vowel. Some students have difficulty with this type of drill, especially with nonsense words; if so, do not stress.

KEY: pass, tiff, sill, spill, still, fill, staff, stiff, dill, lass, nill, till, sniff.

TT   KEY (nonsense – to test application of the rule):

siff, tilf, nass, pilf, saff

4. Spelling: (Watch for i - l reversals.)

1. fip	4. flip	7. fast	10. snaps
2. tans	5. pass	8. slid	11. tilt
3. dill	6. aft	9. flint	12. staff

if it is; a fast fist; as it flips; if it is last; Pat spills a pill. Sniff a plant.

33

Page 8

1. Add h - <u>house</u> (h) and hard g - <u>goat</u> (g) reading cards, both regular. Practice for reading.
2. Add spelling cards (h) and (g) to spelling review pack. Spelling list is after page 9.

Page 9

1. Add ng - <u>king</u> (ng) for reading and spelling.
2. Note that all words given in columns with -<u>ing</u> as suffix are *base* words (complete words) plus -<u>ing</u>. Emphasize this structure to develop concept of suffix.
3. Spelling:

1. gad	4. flag	7. gilt	10. lifting
2. hint	5. gang	8. sting	
3. tang	6. sanding*	9. gasp	

   a passing* fad; slinging a pan

   *Be sure the student spells the baseword as a unit and the suffix as a unit; <u>pass</u> doubles <u>s</u> according to rule, then -<u>ing</u> added.
4. In reading sentences at bottom of page, student should prepare by reading through silently, working out attack problems, so that oral reading is phrased, smooth, and natural.
5. WORKBOOK – page 81 – determining if <u>ing</u> is a suffix in a word.
   KEY:
   Words with suffix: passing, hissing, gasping, lifting, hinting, sifting, planting, panting, ganging, tilting, hanging, sniffing
6. Note at the bottom of page 81 the concept of leading up to the 1-1-1 double spelling rule to be covered in Level VII. The emphasis here is on needing two consonants after a short vowel before adding <u>ing</u>.
   KEY:
   spassing, tasting, snaffing, flisping, spilfing, spinging, pilping, fanting, difting

Page 10

1. Add o - <u>octopus</u> (ŏ), regular for reading and spelling. (<u>a</u> is *not* the regular spelling of (ŏ) - <u>hot</u>.) Difficult for some students. Use nonsense words to ensure sound is secure. Add the *Phono-Cards*.
2. List at right of page is a common variant sound of short <u>o</u>; do *not* include it as a card response or stress. Have students read down this list to make sure they can read the words; most are familiar and cause no problems.

3. Spelling:

1. plod	4. tong	7. loss	10. dolls
2. spot	5. ponds	8. spring	
3. hissing	6. hangs	9. planting	

spill off a log; as a top dog; stop on a soft spot

Page 11

1. Add <u>m</u> - <u>mitten</u> (m) and <u>r</u> - <u>rabbit</u> (r), both regular. Add the reading and spelling cards. The <u>r</u> will be used here only *before* a vowel since it alters sound of vowel if after.

2. Spelling:

1. rid	4. tamp	7. plot	10. grasp
2. mop	5. drill	8. doff	11. limping past
3. tram	6. slim	9. rift	12. grill a ham

Sam is an imp. Ron drags a mop.

3. WORKBOOK – page 6 – unscrambling of <u>ff</u>, <u>ll</u>, <u>ss</u> words and spelling from phonetic pictures.

KEY:

doll, floss, miff, ass, mill, miss, trill;

loll, hiss, gaff, gross, drill, priss, grill

KEY for spelling:

TT frill, mass, golf, doff;

spoff, olf, goss, noll, alf, aff

Pages 12-14

1. Be sure students can read and spell "of, the, Mr., Mrs." at the top of sentences. Use Techniques 4 and 5 if not.

2. Practice in sentence reading will vary according to teacher assessment of student needs. Remind them to read the sentence silently before reading aloud to insure smoothness; only after a student proves he can read smoothly and correctly without such preparation should it be dropped.

Pages 15-16

1. Add <u>e</u> - <u>edge</u> (ĕ), regular for reading and spelling; add both cards. Troublesome for some students, so stress key word learning. Dialectic differences may

cause auditory discrimination problems, especially with (ĭ) in some locales.

2. It is sometimes safer to practice the *e* words on page 16 before the minimal pairs on page 15 for dialectic reasons. Remember to read pairs on 15 *across* for discrimination.

3. The auditory discrimination between (ĕ) and (ĭ) before an <u>m</u> or <u>n</u> is particularly difficult, and the teacher should examine her own pronunciation and choose words carefully for spelling. Some students say the <u>en</u> and <u>in</u> combinations alike and are emotional about changing. Do not stress this group if so.

4. Spelling:

1. fed	4. rang	7. gram	10. lift
2. his	5. sell	8. sleds	11. left
3. lest	6. pomp	9. fret	12. drops

left at the mill; a tan pelt; Ted sits on the net. Pam has lots of pep.

Page 16 – right column

1. Concept: Letters at top (VC´/CV) stand for letter pattern (vowel-consonant-accented syllable-syllable division-then consonant-vowel). Syllable division in this pattern is regularly between the two consonants, thereby *closing* the first syllable and making it a *short* vowel. The syllable division is thus indicating how the vowel is pronounced. (TT)

2. Concept of accent. Explain it as the stress or force given a syllable; the accented syllable is said plainer and louder, usually with a higher tone of voice and the mouth open wider.

   a. Practice shifting accent; have students say the alphabet accenting every *other* letter, then every *third* letter.

   b. Read to students a list of three-syllable words and have them pick out the syllable being accented (like: astronaut, volcano, Cadillac, student, among, police).

   c. Some students cannot detect accent auditorily without exaggerated practice. Teacher discretion on how much.

3. Note difference in accent in words at bottom of column.

4. Remember a one-syllable word is accented; if it is a closed syllable, the vowel is short; if it is open (<u>me</u>), the vowel is long.

5. *Page 63* in Workbook done after reading practice on 16. Practice in dividing syllables in VCCV pattern, determining and marking the accent after reading and noting pattern; student gets visual reinforcement of letter pat-

tern determining the sound of the vowel. (TT)

KEY:

TT   ăd/mĭt´, Dăl´/lăs, pŏs/sĕss´, ĭn´/fănt, sĕl´/dŏm, dĕn´/tĭst, ăs/sĭst´, ĕr´/rănd*, găl´/lŏn, ăr/rĕst´*, săn´/dăl

        *if the student knows and tries the (âr) or (ĕr) sounds in these words, point out that a <u>double r</u> following the vowel does not change the vowel sound; it maintains its regular short sound in a closed syllable.

Page 17 (and left of 18)

1. Words of the two accent patterns are mixed. Student gets practice dividing the syllables orally and can try the accent on each syllable in turn and choose the word sounding familiar to him. Remember short vowel before <u>rr</u>! Individualize amount.

2. Compliment correct pronunciation of words obviously never learned by the student, strengthening his realization that he is applying learned concepts in word attack.

3. Words in the VCCV pattern regular for spelling with the phonograms already covered can now be included for spelling if carefully chosen for short sounds in both syllables. Choose only words with two different consonants in VCCV at this point in training. In dictating words for spelling exaggerate the short vowel sounds; do *not* give the unaccented (ə) vowel sound.

4. Sample spelling:

1. mantis	4. raglan	a red pigment
2. stopgap	5. distant	admit the gang
3. figment	6. hamlet	

Page 18 – right column

1. A consonant blend sticks together in a syllable and behaves as one consonant. Do not overstress the division with three consonants; many students have no problem reading these blends. If there is difficulty, be sure not to include for spelling.

2. Workbook – *page 64* (top section) – use according to student ability and needs.

TT   KEY:

     im/press´, Al´/fred, trans/mit´
     in´/stant, pil´/grim, mis´/tress

1. Concept of <u>consonant y</u>. Most students can read <u>y</u> at the beginning of a word but may have problem with the isolated response to the card and have confusion with vowel <u>y</u>.

2. <u>Y</u> is a consonant as the initial letter in a base word (<u>yarn</u>, <u>yes</u>) and at the beginning of a few syllables (<u>law yer</u>, <u>can yon</u>). Otherwise <u>y</u> will be a vowel (see 4 below).

3. Consonant <u>y</u> is regular for reading (y) and for spelling the sound (y) at the beginning of base words. Add the reading card and the spelling card for consonant <u>y</u>. A few exceptions for spelling the sound within a word, are span<u>ie</u>l, Ital<u>ia</u>n, jun<u>io</u>r. Do not bring up these exceptions now with student.

4. Introduce the vowel <u>y</u>. Note that there is a consonant <u>y</u> card and a vowel <u>y</u> reading card, which should now be added. The response to the reading card is <u>yarn</u> (y); respond <u>candy</u> (ĭ) and <u>fly</u> (ī) to the vowel card. The teacher should have the following information in mind before introducing vowel-<u>y</u> and share it with students according to need.

  TT   a. <u>Y</u> is another way of *spelling* <u>i</u>; therefore it has the long and short sounds of <u>i</u> in English.

        b. English words do not usually end in <u>i</u> spelling, so <u>y</u> is the regular spelling at the *end* of a word for (ĭ) and (ī). (<u>ski</u> is Norwegian, <u>taxi</u> is shortened <u>taxicab</u>, <u>hi</u> a contraction.)

        c. In some dialects, and increasingly in common speech, the unaccented final <u>y</u> is pronounced (ē) instead of (ĭ), and this makes for confusion in spelling. Pronounce it short in reading exercises to ingrain concept of final <u>y</u> and for spelling dictation.

        d. If the <u>y</u> is accented, as in one-syllable words (<u>try</u>) or (<u>fly</u>), it is long because of the open, accented syllable. Practice word picture with this
  TT   concept (trī).

        e. A final vowel *y* can be part of the base word, as in the first two sections on 19-20, or a *suffix* meaning "full of" added to a base word and usually making the word an adjective (<u>sandy</u>). Suffix <u>y</u> is never accented or long in sound.

        f. Do not get involved here with the rule for doubling the consonant when adding the suffix <u>y</u>. Words in the Study Book do not include such words, as <u>sunny</u>, for this reason, but they usually will present no problems for reading

        g. The vowel <u>y</u> in the middle of a base word is from the Greek language, and the words are usually scientific or medical. This offers a visual clue for context. If necessary, the student can usually mentally substitute an i̱ in place of the y̱ for reading such words and follow the pattern for long and short sounds. Do not dwell on the medial *y* examples at the bottom of 20; make the point that they are from the Greek and can be read as though the y̱ were i̱.

    h. Remember y̱ is the regular spelling for the sound (ĭ) or (ī) at the *end* of a word. Any other spelling with the vowel y̱ is irregular and must be learned.

5. Add the response "at the end of a word – y̱" to the spelling card for (ĭ) after (ĭ) – i̱. Do not add the spelling card for the long i̱ yet even though it is here presented regular for spelling at the end of a short word (tr̲y̲).

6. Spelling:

1. yip	4. fry	7. dandy	10. frilly
2. yell	5. spry	8. nifty	11. smelly
3. yon	6. ply	9. pansy	12. drafty

plenty of drilling; a grassy spot; fifty prints

Tests I-A and I-B and I-1 and I-2 in Appendix can be given at this point for evaluation.

Pages 21-22

1. Introduce u̱ - u̲p̲ (ŭ). Regular for reading and spelling; add the respective cards. Practice lists move from simplest to complex. The unaccented (ə) sound given open syllables may have confused students in the past about spelling.

2. The student can count on spelling (ŭ) with a u̱ when he hears an accented closed syllable. The other response to the spelling card will come later.

3. Spelling:

1. pug	4. slump	7. ugly	in a huff
2. gulf	5. gruff	8. insult	plums and figs
3. drum	6. rusty	fungus on a stump	

A yam is a spud. A mustang is not a nag.

Page 23

1. These nonsense syllables make an excellent review and evaluation for pages 4-22 for reading and spelling. Explain to student that these could be real syllables in real words.

2. Do not use any nonsense words with a medial y for spelling since this is not regular (i would be regular in middle).

Pages 24-25

1. Learn regular words to and do by Techniques 4 and 5 if student doesn't know them. What would be the regular pronunciation of these words? (tō and dō)
2. First chance to read paragraphs aloud for practice. Use according to individualized needs.

Page 26

1. Introduce k - kite (k) and nk - sink (ngk) for reading. Practice.
2. Note that except for skull, k is not used in these words before an a, o, or u (only an e, i, or y). This will be important for spelling when c is introduced next. Hold off on (k) for spelling until c is introduced.

Pages 27-28

1. Introduce c - cup (k), for reading.
2. Note that the (k) sound only appears before a, o, or u vowels in these words and is spelled c.
3. Practice until pronunciation of the words from these pages is secure.
4. Introduce the (k) card for spelling. The response is "(k) - c, k before e, i, or y." Do not include the ck response yet.
TT 5. Introduce the concept that the spelling of (k) depends on letters around it. Before an e, i, or y at the beginning or in the middle of a word, (k) is spelled k. Before the other vowels (a, o, u) and consonants, the regular spelling is c. Many more words begin with c than k when (k); count pages in dictionary if student is not convinced. They should "think c" unless they cannot use c for the forthcoming reason.
6. Spelling:

1. skit	4. cop	7. keg
2. cram	5. yet	8. clip
3. cuff	6. camp	9. risky

Page 29 – left

The combination -ct at the end of a word is difficult to say distinctly. Practice with that in mind.

1. Introduce the (s) sound for <u>c</u>, which is regular for reading before an <u>e</u>, <u>i</u>, or <u>y</u> (very few exceptions: <u>soccer</u>). Response to the <u>c</u> reading card should be "cup - (k), (s) before <u>e</u>, <u>i</u>, or <u>y</u>."

2. Students read the 3rd and 4th columns on p. 29. Additional practice lists could be made like: crib, cent, cut, crust, fancy, cactus, classic, accept.

3. IMPORTANT: the (s) sound of <u>c</u> is not regular for spelling except between a vowel and <u>e</u>, <u>i</u>, or <u>y</u> (*face*); do *not* add this response yet. Otherwise it must be a learned spelling.

4. It should become apparent to the student there is a reason (k) must be spelled <u>k</u> in front of an <u>e</u>, <u>i</u>, or <u>y</u> (a <u>c</u> would have to be pronounced (s) when read back.) The student must discriminate the sound that follows the (k) to know which letter to spell with.

5. Add the spelling card (ngk) - <u>nk</u>. <u>K</u> is the regular spelling as the last letter for (k) at the end of one-syllable words with consonant -(k); (si<u>nk</u>, not sin<u>c</u>, is regular).

6. Spelling:

1. sank	4. crest	7. cling
2. plunk	5. napkin	8. gasket
3. cliff	6. elk	9. kings

   The sun sinks. Fling the plank.

7. WORKBOOK – *pages 9-11*

   a. *Page 9* – Practice on visually recognizing the letter following <u>c</u> which determines its sound, and then writing that sound picture. The letter <u>c</u> has no sound of its own and is either (k) or (s) in sound pictures. This exercise could be done orally, only giving the sound for <u>c</u>, or words could be read.
   KEY:
   TT Top, by columns: (1) k, s, k, k; k, s, s, k.
   Nonsense by columns: (1) s, k, s, k, s, k, k; (2) s, k, s, s, k, k, s; (3) s, k, s, k, s, k, s.

   b. *Page 10* – Supplying the letter <u>c</u> or <u>k</u> for spelling in the blank as determined by the letter following. Read completed words aloud.
   KEY:
   TT 1st column: *cap*, c, k, c, k, c, k, c, k, c, c, k, k, c, c, c, k;
   2nd: k, c, c, c, k, c, c, k, k, c, c, k, k, c, c, c, k.

3rd (nonsense): k, c, k, c, k, c, c, c, c, c, k, c, c, k, c, k, c;

4th: k, c, c, c, k, c, k, c, c, k, k, c, c, c, k, c, c.

c. *Page 11* – Students copy the generalization on (k) (at top of page) in notebook. Dictate the following words for student to write spelling in proper c̲ or k̲ column:

TT   (Mix order when dictating): Under c̲up̲: cult, scat, crop, candid, cutlet, contest, scum, infect, clasp. Under k̲ip̲: Keds, kiss, skid, sulky, king, kept, kid, skill, kelp.

Pages 30

TT   1. This page of nonsense words should be utilized according to needs. The syllables are short but will probably require real thought and practice.

2. Stress that in s̲ce̲, s̲ci̲, or s̲cy̲, only one (s) is pronounced.

Pages 31

1. Introduce c̲k̲ - tr̲uck̲ (k) for reading. Note that the (k) is just said once even though both letters have the (k) sound.

2. Read top of page for discovery that the (k) is only spelled c̲k̲ when *immediately after* a short vowel. It is a spelling convention and should present no problem for reading.

3. In the 4th column, teacher might note that d̲errick̲, l̲ipstick̲, and g̲immick̲ are exceptions to AA spelling principle for -i̲c̲ at end.

4. When the c̲ and k̲ spelling generalization is thoroughly secure, add c̲k̲ as the 3rd spelling response to the (k) card: "(k)-c̲; k̲ before e̲, i̲, or y̲; and c̲k̲." The generalization, to be copied in notebook is: "Use c̲k̲ at the end of a one-syllable word *immediately* after a short vowel."

5. Spelling:

1. rock	4. cast	7. pink	10. tricky
2. sink	5. speck	8. pick	11. crank
3. tack	6. mock	9. task	12. lucky

6. WORKBOOK – *page 12* – Individualize amount needed. Applying the above generalization by noting the letter pattern of short vowel before *ck*.

TT   KEY:

1st column: sack, ck, k, k, ck, ck, ck, k, ck, k, ck, k, k;

2nd: sank, k, ck, ck, k, k, k, ck, k, ck, k, ck, ck;

3rd: ck, ck, ck, ck, k, ck, ck, k, ck, ck, k, ck, ck;

4th: k, k, k, k, ck, k, k, ck, k, k, ck, k, k.

TT *Page 13* KEY:
   1st: stock, k, k, ck, ck, k, ck, ck, k, ck, ck, k, ck, ck;
   2nd: ck, k, k, k, k, k, k, k, ck, k, k, ck, ck, k;
   Nonsense 3rd: k, ck, k, ck, ck, ck, k, k, ck, ck, ck, k, ck, k;
   4th: ck, k, ck, ck, k, k, ck, ck, ck, k, k, k, k, ck.

TT *Page 14* – May be confusing to some students; skip it if so. Others like this
   type as puzzle.
   KEY:
   1st: duck, lock, luck, tack, neck, sack, rock, lick, kick, pick;
   2nd: truck, stuck, smack, clock, trick, track, fleck, crack, click, speck.

TT *Page 15* – Because this page includes the generalization of (ĭk), it may be
   considered advanced.
   KEY:
   1st col.: attic, neck, dusk, plastic, flank, tannic, track, aspic, hunk, metric,
   stuck, classic, deck.
   2nd: prick, mystic, stank, optic, fleck, Celtic, tuck, task, lactic, styptic, flick,
   hectic, frantic.
   3rd: slink, picnic, slack, cosmic, sulk, rink, mastic, puck, citric, lank,
   skeptic, traffic, muck.

   7. Demonstrate again that the sound picture of <u>c</u> is either (k) or (s). <u>C</u> has no
   sound of its own!

Page 32

   1. Practice in reading the pairs of sentences smoothly.
   2. Sentences 1, 2, 5, 6, and 7 can be dictated for spelling to more able students.

Pages 33-34

   1. Introduce <u>b</u> - <u>bat</u> (b), regular for reading and spelling. Add both cards. Be
   sure the student does not respond (bŭ). Watch for reversals in reading or
   spelling with <u>d</u> or <u>p</u> and give multi-sensory practice in discrimination if they
   appear.
   2. Students will probably only need to read parts of these columns.
   3. Spelling:

1. rob	4. bid	7. brink	10. tablet
2. club	5. bunt	8. stub	11. goblet
3. brag	6. black	9. bask	12. bandit

   a bell on a belt; bluffing Bob; a grab bag

Page 35

1. Introduce j – jam (j), regular for reading; add the *Phono-Card*. J is never doubled or the final letter in English words.

2. J for spelling is regular at the beginning or middle of a base word before an a, o, or u. Add the (j) spelling card. Response to the card (j) now is j. Do not stress because of the limited use of j in English words. *G* will later be introduced as the most common spelling of (j), before an e, i, or y.

3. Introduce final o, long in an open accented syllable. Most of these words are from Spanish, Mexican, or Italian. Pronunciation of the final o is rarely a problem, and it is *not* given as a reading card response. Do not use the final o words for spelling drills since o is not the regular English spelling for (ō) at the end of words; ow is.

4. WORKBOOK – *page 21* – the important reading concept of a long vowel at the end of a one-syllable word in contrast to the short vowel in a closed syllable. Good kinesthetic reinforcement to an essential understanding.

5. Make sure that students know that a long vowel says its name and they learn the sound pictures: (ā), (ē), (ī), etc. The long mark is properly called a macron (mā´kron).

6. Students should learn as a chant and repeat it daily until the concept is secure:

   "A vowel at the end of an unaccented syllable is long.

   A vowel in a closed syllable is short."

Page 36

Extra practice in syllable division of VCCV pattern, extended to 3-syllable words. For more able students, the following could be dictated for spelling: dentistry, amnesty, inconstant, malcontent.

Pages 37-38

To be used for individual needs.

Page 39

1. Have students read down each of three columns of -ed words at top of the page before introducing -ed to see if they can detect sounds they are giving it.

2. Introduce the suffix ed for reading. This -ed can be read three ways, depending upon the consonant immediately preceding it. The response to the read-

ing ed card, which is now added, is "folded - (ĕd), jumped - (t), sailed - (d)." This usually presents few problems for reading except for the tendency of some students to read all ed endings (ĕd). It is pronounced as a separate syllable (ĕd) only immediately after a d or a t as the final letter of the base word. A few adjectives are exceptions although these need not be presented now: aged, blessed, crooked, dogged, jagged, learned, ragged, rugged, and beloved.

3. Auditory discrimination training may be used to help a student understand when a final (d) or (t) sound is the suffix -ed added to a base word. This

TT concept is important for spelling. *Say* these words, repeating without the final (d) or (t) to determine if a whole base word is left:

land	banged	went	jumped
hint	sniffed	command	dulled
blast	stamped		

This can be especially confusing to some students when the final sound is (kt). Words like tact and tacked must be given in context to be able to determine spelling. Practice for auditory discrimination, said as above:

| fact | locked | suspect | tricked |
| compact | flunked | | |

4. Add ed as the second response to spelling cards (t) and (d). Response will now be (t): "(t), t and ed."

5. WORKBOOK – *pages 82-90* – at teacher discretion.

   Page 82 – This page gives visual emphasis to the concept that the *ed* is being read in one of three possible ways and is the foundation for spelling words with -ed suffixes. If a student has natural ability to read -ed words correctly,

TT do not allow this approach to confuse him.
   KEY:
   1. t; 2. d; 3. ed; 4. d; 5. t; 6. t; 7. ed; 8. t; 9. d; 10. t; 11. ed; 12. t; 13. t; 14. d; 15. ed; 16. t; 17. d.

   Page 83 – Translating visual sound pictures into the spelling of the word:
   KEY:
   2. drilled, yelled; 3. bumped, spilled; 4. socked; 5. fussed, hissed; 6. picked; 7. kissed, licked; 8. smacked; 9. jumped, cracked; 10. blinked.

   Page 84 – involves understanding of -ing as the progressive form after is or

TT kept, and ed as the past tense suffix with yesterday or has. Stress spelling of whole base word, then adding the suffix.
   KEY:
   2. yelping, yelped; 3. sniffing, smelled; 4. packed, packing; 5. picking,

picked; 6. passed, backing; 7. pressed, pressing.

AA *Pages 85-87* – Require more understanding than many students develop. Omit these pages if desired. These words must be used in context if dictated.

Page 85 – Base word in left column, base word and suffix in right.
KEY:

past, passed; mist, missed; tract, tracked; tact, tacked; mast, massed; duct, ducked; pact, packed; must, mussed.

AA *Page 86*
KEY:

mist, missed; past, passed; tacked, tact; ducked, duct; pact, packed; tracked, tract; massed, mast; must, mussed.

AA *Page 87*
KEY:

1. tucked, locked; 2. strict, yanked; 3. masked, flanked; 4. flocked, tricked; 5. mocked, kicked; 6. backed, banked; 7. cracked, suspect.

Page 88 – This page reinforces the concepts of base word plus suffix, formation of adjectives, and meaning in suffixes. It is valuable drill and does require some thinking about meaning.

TT KEY:

2. helpless; 3. hatless; 4. trustful; 5. fretful; 6. restless; 7. cupful; 8. topless; 9. restful; 10. skinless.

Page 89 – Reinforcement of the spelling concept, (without stating the rule), of a base word plus a suffix beginning with a consonant.
KEY:

justly, stiffness, fondly, sickness, stillness, gruffly, helpfully, distinctly, fastness.

TT *Page 90* – Reinforcement of the concept of a suffix added to a base word. Copy words with suffixes and circle the suffix. If the student cannot copy accurately, omit the exercise.
KEY:

Words containing suffixes: sandy, milky, drafty, crispy, dusty, hilly, jumpy, lucky, pesty; kissed, inked, acted, ended, added, filled, skilled, yelped, pecked, lasted, huffed, jelled, milked; fitness, silken, skillful, costly, sagless, fastness, sicken, sinful, petless, fondly, glassful, flatness, sunless, stiffen, rimless.

TT 6. Spelling:

1. planted	4. yelled	7. sanded	10. gruffly
2. camped	5. blocked	8. skinless	11. redness
3. bunked	6. filmed`	9. misty	12. fretful

Page 40

1. Add <u>w</u> - <u>wig</u> (w) card for reading; <u>w</u> has no sound by itself but is formed by the rounding of the lips with the sound coming from the following vowel.

2. The <u>w</u> is regular for spelling (w) at the beginning of a base word, except as (kw) - <u>qu</u>, and is never doubled. Add the spelling card.

3. Spelling:

1. well	4. swift	7. swanky	10. wed
2. twisted	5. twenty	8. west	
3. wetness	6. willing	9. swing	

4. Add <u>wa</u> - <u>watch</u> (wŏ), card for reading. An <u>a</u> following an initial <u>w</u> takes on the continental <u>a</u> sound (ŏ) in a number of words, and this pronunciation for <u>wa</u> should be the first choice for an unfamiliar word.

5. Add (wŏ), <u>wa</u> as a spelling card and regular spelling.

6. Spelling:

1. wad	2. swat	3. wasp

   swab the deck; I want a wand.

Page 41

1. Introduce <u>v</u> - <u>vest</u> (v), regular for reading and spelling. Add both cards. <u>F</u> and <u>v</u> are a voiced and unvoiced pair, and some students display confusion between them in reading and/or spelling.

2. Note that English words do not end in <u>v</u>, but in <u>ve</u>; <u>v</u> is never doubled.

3. The final <u>ive</u> is pronounced (ĭv) and is regular for spelling when it is a *suffix*.

Page 42

1. Add <u>z</u> - <u>zebra</u> (z), regular for reading; add the *Phono-Card*. A <u>zz</u> is, of course, pronounced only once (z).

2. To the spelling card responses add the <u>z</u> spelling for (z), regular only at the beginning of a base word. The regular spelling for (z) in other positions is <u>s</u>. Response to (z) is now "<u>s</u>, <u>z</u>."

3. Spelling:

1. velvet	4. invest	7. zips
2. vats	5. solve	8. twelve
3. solvent	6. zest	

4. Add <u>x</u> (ks), regular for reading but difficult for some students to pronounce in an unfamiliar word. Add the reading card <u>x</u>. X is never doubled nor used at the beginning of real English words. Coined words like <u>Exxon</u> and <u>X-ray</u> are exceptions; and initial <u>x</u>, when found is pronounced (z), as in <u>Xerox</u>.

Page 43

1. The division in pronunciation of <u>x</u> indicated in columns 2 and 3 should not be emphasized to confuse students who are able to pronounce the <u>x</u>. The (gz) sound, as in <u>exam</u>, is the voiced form. It need not be given as a response to the reading card on the Skills Level but should be by more advanced students.

2. The prefix <u>ex</u>, meaning "out of", is a common English prefix and should be called to students' attention.

3. For spelling, the <u>x</u> is the regular spelling of (ks) in the prefixes <u>ex</u> and <u>extra</u> and in base words, particularly on the end of a word that is singular in meaning. Add the spelling card (ks) - <u>x</u>. (The (gz)-<u>x</u> card is added for the Advanced Level.) An <u>s</u> is very rarely used immediately after an <u>x</u>. The (s) sound heard is from the <u>x</u>. In derivative words when the final sound is (ks), the student will need to recognize the situation as that of a base word plus ending (<u>cooks</u>, <u>takes</u>, <u>kicks</u>, <u>attics</u>) and spell the base word ending in (k) according to the generalization for final (k), plus the <u>s</u>. This is another opportunity to establish understanding of base words and the function of suffixes.

TT

4. Spelling:

1. fix	4. convex	7. extent	10. expel*
2. wax	5. expand	8. exam	
3. next	6. Texas*	9. an index	

*Do not double last letter <u>s</u> or <u>l</u>; these words have two syllables.
a brass sax; at the exit; a box of mix

Page 44-45

1. The paragraphs offer good oral practice. The football is pictured because the <u>oo</u> and <u>all</u> in <u>football</u> have not yet been covered. Read # as "number."

48

3. Practice on 45 points out <u>ed</u> suffix in multisyllable words. Read across to emphasize differences in pronunciation of <u>ed</u>.

Page 46

1. Introduce <u>qu</u> - <u>queen</u> (kw), regular for reading and spelling in base words. Add both cards. This pronunciation is difficult for some students. The letter <u>q</u> is rarely used in English words without <u>u</u>. The <u>u</u> is not considered a vowel in this combination but is treated as though it were the consonant <u>w</u>.

2. The <u>qua</u> (kwŏ) is the same situation as the <u>wa</u> (wŏ) on page 40, and that page should be reviewed. It is the <u>w</u> lip shape that changes the <u>a</u> pronunciation in many, but not all, <u>qua</u> words. It may be advisable to omit the nonsense words with asterisks to avoid confusion in some students.

3. The questions at the bottom of column 3 are seeking recognition that the <u>ll</u>, <u>ff</u>, and <u>ck</u> signal one short vowel sound immediately preceding (<u>qu</u> is considered as two consonants).

4. There are a few foreign words, (<u>mosquito</u>, <u>liquor</u>, <u>mosque</u>), where <u>qu</u> has the (k) sound; these should be taught as learned words when needed.

5. Spelling: Remember to emphasize that <u>qu</u> acts as two consonants. (This will also be important in determining later spelling situations such as <u>quitter</u>.)

1. quit	4. quicksand	7. squat
2. quack	5. inquest	8. squad
3. quill	6. banquet	

6. WORKBOOK - *pages 16-17* – With teacher discretion. If these exercises prove too difficult for students with limited vocabulary or ability, omit them.

   TT KEY:

   1. obstruct, constrict; 2. subject; 3. district; 4. neglect; 5. contact, instruct; 6. insect, infect; 7. inspect, suspect; 8. convict; 9. distinct; 10. conduct; 11. distract; 12. concoct; 13. contract, construct; 14. extinct; 15. expect, conflict; 16. impact, compact

7. WORKBOOK – *page 22* – Review the sound picture, for sounds learned to this point: (Teacher may need to help students work this out.) Long vowel sound are included even though only briefly covered to date.

   KEY: (t), (p), (n), (s) (z), (ă) (ā), (l), (d), (f), (h), (g), (ng), (ŏ) (ō), (m), (r), (ĕ) (ē), (y), (ĭ) (ī), (ŭ) (ū), (k), (k) (s), (k), (b), (j), (ĕd) (t) (d), (w), (v), (kw), (ks) (gz), (z).

8. WORKBOOK – *page 23*

   a. This is the regular, most common spelling of a single consonant sound after a short vowel in two syllable words. These words can be referred to as "rabbit" words. Have all students read through the top lists and call the spelling to their attention. Students should copy this spelling situation in notebooks.

    b. Auditory training to discriminate "rabbit" words is valuable. Teacher may read the following lists aloud and students decide if each word is a "rabbit word" with a double consonant. "Do you hear only *one* consonant sound after a short vowel? Then the double consonant is the regular spelling." Say:

TT

object	bonnet*	muskrat	elbow
combine	trellis*	jello*	manner*
tunnel*	trinket	putty*	fossils*
frantic	common*	trombone	dentist

AA   c. KEY:

carrot, muslin, marry, connect, album, parrot, correct, brandy, gallop; holly, hoblet, barrel, tunnel, baptist, sudden, gully, gallon, bonnet, hobby

    d. Spelling dictation:

1. happy	4. silly	7. carrot	10. berry
2. possum	5. blanket	8. daffy	
3. album	6. puppet	9. mascot	

  9. WORKBOOK – *page 24*

AA KEY:

fry, yell, clock, swan, have, sly, box, quill, swamp, solve, quick, tuck, squat, live, concoct, expect, conquest, object, candy, extract, involve, clumsy, expand, insect, extend, fifty, extinct, wisdom.

Page 47

Practice in blending base words with two suffixes, reinforcing the view of the suffix as a familiar unit.

Page 48

Two-syllable nonsense words. These can be used as evaluation for more able students. Omit with the severely disabled

Page 49-55

Practice reading material. Amount used to be determined by individual needs.

TT
1. These exercises may be done orally, without underlining. They involve considerable vocabulary knowledge and ability to categorize; they are excellent for those able to do them.

2. *Page 55*

   KEY:

   2. magnet; 3. Preston; 4. spitting; 5. class; 6. Larry; 7. Dallas; 8. Pam; 9. swelling; 10. elk; 11. ill; 12. strum; 13. sky; 14. pencils. Pictures: the glass

3. *Page 56*

   KEY:

   2. floss; 3. mittens; 4. pond; 5. rust; 6. swamp; 7. pans; 8. back; 9. barrel; 10. disk; 11. lob; 12. brass; 13. legs; 14. trump. Letters – the A (vowel.)

Level II

Level II tests for reading and for spelling are located in the Appendix for evaluation purposes.

Sample behavioral objectives for Level II:

Upon the completion of Level II for reading training:

1. When presented with the 6 reading cards for the vowel-consonant-silent e pattern (a-e, e-e, i-e, o-e, u-e, y-e), the student must be able to respond orally with the key word and long vowel sound for each card with 100 percent accuracy.

2. When presented with Test II-A list of 20 words containing only letter patterns, phonograms, and concepts covered in Levels I and II of *Angling for Words*, the student will demonstrate his ability to read the list orally with 90 percent accuracy.

3. When presented with test II-B, list of 10 nonsense words containing only phonograms and patterns stressed in Level II of *Angling*, the student will demonstrate his ability to read the list orally with 80 percent accuracy.

Upon completion of Level II for spelling:

1. When presented with the oral long sounds of five vowels, (ā), (ē), (ī), (ō), (ū), the student will demonstrate the ability to repeat the sound and make the proper oral response of "a-consonant-e, e-consonant-e," etc., spelling the sound with 100 percent accuracy.

51

2. Upon dictation of Test II-1 list of 10 words for spelling, covering only phonograms, concepts, and patterns covered in Levels I or II, the student shall demonstrate his understanding of the vowel-consonant-e pattern of spelling long vowel sound by writing the correct spelling of at least 8 words.

3. The student, upon dictation of the Test II-2 list of 8 nonsense words, shall demonstrate his understanding of the vowel-consonant-e pattern of spelling long vowel sounds by writing the correct spelling of at least 6 words.

Page 58

Read carefully the concepts to be reviewed which are listed in the *Preparation* and the concepts to be developed in Level II in reading and in spelling. Note that the a-e symbols are read, "a (or vowel)-consonant-e."

Page 59

1. Review the concept of a long vowel in an open accented syllable (introduced with y on page 19 of the Study Book) and the closed syllable with the short vowel.

2. Introduce the concept of the silent e being added to a closed syllable and changing the vowel pronunciation to long (saying its letter name.) Except for monosyllables with final e the only vowel (he, she, me, etc.), the final e in English words is usually silent. However, there must be only *one* vowel and *one* consonant and a silent e to signal this long vowel pattern visually.

3. Note that the long u, which regularly is pronounced as the letter name u, may be altered to an (o͞o) sound after l, r, or s.

4. Read the third group in horizontal pairs for auditory and visual contrast.

5. In the a r e words in the center section a is treated and marked as any v-r-e word although the r alters the long sound of the a somewhat: care (kãr).

6. WORKBOOK – *page 25* – Practice in recognizing the visual clue of the v-con-e letter pattern to know that the vowel in such patterns is long. If there are *two* consonants before the e, the vowel will usually not be long.

   WORKBOOK – *pages 26, 27, 28* – The contrasting pairs are spelled for the student and are to be placed into the sentences using context for meaningful sentences. The completed sentences should be read aloud.

TT KEY:

   ate, at; slid, slide; kit, kite; fill, file; fad, fade; hope, hop; duke, duck; plan, plane; pal, pale; snack, snake; cub, cube; fate, fat; cocks, cokes; like, lick;

hates, hats; rake, rack; quit, quite; pick, pike; Tim, time; Pete, pet; quake, quack; sit, site; dine, din; tricks, trikes; tot, tote.

Page 60

1. Students read groups of 3 contrasting patterns horizontally to reinforce recognition of the patterns.
2. The list in column 4 is read vertically.

Page 61-62

1. These minimal pairs in mixed order make excellent practice material to strengthen the concept of v-con-e; the amount used for practice should be individualized by need.
2. For students with great difficulty mastering this pattern, work may also be begun on Level III while Level II practice continues. Even for more able students, it is often advantageous to begin Level III as Level II practice progresses in small sections for longer reinforcement; the concepts in the two levels do not usually become confused.

Page 63

1. Add the six vowel-con-*e* reading cards to the daily pack. Response given is "cake - (ā), athlete (ē)." etc. Note that the u-con-e card has two responses to be given now, the pronunciation of the u depending on the preceding consonant.
2. Students read the words in all sections horizontally for contrasting patterns. The visual spelling contrasts combine with the long and short vowel auditory contrasts in oral reading to strengthen the concept of the spelling patterns.

TT
3. The center section of words combines the (k) and (s) sound with the short and long vowel patterns and involves the ce pattern; this group requires careful thought on the part of many students as they read horizontally.
4. WORKBOOK – *page 18*
   a. This is a continuation of previous training in spelling the (k) sound. A (k) after a long vowel sound is spelled regularly ke (as stated on page 19, no. 3).
   b. The exercise demands visual recognition of the mark for the long or short sound of the vowel, which in turn demands either the ke, ck or k

spelling. Teacher choice here might be to have the student read the written vowel sounds aloud to aid in making the choice.

    c. KEY:

(in horizontal pairs) Mack, make; lick, like; hike, hick; smock, smoke; coke, cock; lack, lake; Dick, dike; sack, sake; pike, pick;

duke, duck; jack, Jake; tack, take; rake, rack; stack, stake; quake, quack; stock, stoke; luck, Luke; pock, poke; snake, snack.

Vertically in the bottom section): sank, tusk, rank, milk, brick; fabric, invoke;

track, trick, silk, neck, joke, clambake, Atlantic;

clock, brisk, peck, slack, click;

strike, wake, stuck, lock, struck, mistake, mandrake.

5. WORKBOOK – *page 19*– Review of the generalization of spelling final (k)

TT   listed here. Copy these three parts in notebook.

Dictate the following words in random order for the student to write in the correct column on his paper.

ck column: tack, pick, hack, deck, prick, crock;

k column: task, crank, pink, honk, sulk, frisk;

ke column: pike, stake, smoke, quake, trike, joke;

ic column: frantic, optic, public, metric, Atlantic, fantastic.

6. WORKBOOK – *page 29* – Review and check on understanding of the concept of sound pictures translated into spelling patterns.

AA   KEY:

mill, mile, cock, coke, quake, quack, pile, pill, fluff, cute, sake, sack, spite; snake, snack, cube, cub, glass, lake, stiff, quit, slime, track, squire, quite, smock.

7. WORKBOOK – *page 30*

AA   KEY:

smoke, fill, bass, code, trick, pipe, rake, cane, stuff, quote, stack, flake, pass; fine, made, till, rate, lack, take, bite, time, will, pick, pike, muff, fade.

Page 64

Good evaluation and practice in recognizing the coding patterns for long and short vowel sounds. The amount used should be individualized.

Page 65

1. Practice in two-syllable words with v-con-e; some short vowel patterns are mixed in for discrimination.

2. The regular spelling of a long vowel sound in a final closed syllable is the vowel-consonant-e. Spelling cards should be added now with the second listed response only: (ā) - "a-consonant-e," (ē) - "e-consonant-e," (ī) - "i-consonant-e," (y-con-e is not regular spelling), (ō) - "o-consonant-e," (ū) "u-consonant-e." Do not add the (ōō) spelling card yet. E-con-e is *not* the regular spelling for e in closed monosyllables; (ee is.)

3. Add the second response for the spelling card (s): "s; c between a vowel and e, i, or y" (as in rice).

4. Sample spelling lists:

1. spine	4. clove	7. snake	10. muss
2. grad	5. mute	8. grim	11. jute
3. grade	6. trod	9. probe	12. twine

   a stiff spine; a mile rode; a mode of life

5. WORKBOOK – *page 31* – Good practice for those able to do it. Note the accents on syllables with long vowel sounds.

TT KEY:

AA plate, quill, lick, like, admire, dictate, combine, dispute, victim, invite, explore, extreme, compact, reptile;

Slide, wine, win, same, ignore, expose, injure, invade, stampede, talcum, posture, quintet, expect, confine

Page 66-67

1. Practice in 2 and 3 syllable words, mostly v-con-e but with some short vowels for discrimination. Good practice which gives self-confidence to most students as they realize they can read many unfamiliar words.

2. Spelling:

1. vampire	3. condone	5. impose
2. exhale	4. stagnate	6. compare

   a velvet cape; a strong rope; at a fast rate
   A fad will fade. Dan is a Dane.

55

Nonsense words:

1. sape	4. bune	7. og	10. spon
2. hile	5. lut.	8. nate	
3. plag	6. zope	9. nide	

Pages 68-74

Reading practice with v-consonant-e words in sentences to be used according to individual needs. Good to use in small sections for review as work progresses into Level III.

Page 75

KEY to note at the bottom of the page:

Hi Tim!

The nap by the lone pine on the slope was fun! In the camp games I will toss a plate discus, jump the stick on the pole, and hop in the sack race. Quickly I hope!

Till next time,
Jack

Page 76

1. Words in the top section put the suffixes beginning with consonants on base words with closed syllables.

2. The center section puts these suffixes on v-con-e words. Read across to mix suffixes. The important skill being developed is the students' seeing the base word and the suffix as separate units and therefore responding to the v-con-e visual pattern with the long vowel sound and then adding the familiar suffix. (This prevents pronouncing the silent e as a separate syllable.)

Pages 77-82

Additional practice, amount used to be at teacher's discretion.

Page 83

1. Important practice on v-c-e words with suffixes, strengthening the visual pattern of base word plus suffix.

2. WORKBOOK – *pages 91-92* – Written practice adding the consonant suffixes to v-con-e base words. This involves memory of meaning of the suffixes to fit the context. Be sure completed sentences are read aloud.

KEY:

1. tuneful (not tune<u>less</u>!); 2. nameless; 3. soreness; 4. fineness; 5. useful;
6. rarely; 7. pureness; 8. homeless; 9. jokeful; 10. safely; 11. smileless;
12. bravely, carefully; 13. blameful; 14. blameless; 15. graceful; 16. tamely;
17. baseless (could be <u>baseful</u>); 18. wakeful; 19. gamely.

Page 84

1. Excellent discrimination review of the patterns with suffixes. Better go slow-ly! This presents a good opportunity to call students' attention to how much difference in meaning one letter can make in similar words. (hats - hates)

2. Spelling: A consonant suffix does not change the spelling of the base word. (This does not apply, however, to base words ending in <u>y</u>, a spelling rule not yet studied.)

1. gravely	4. robes	7. lameness
2. cāreful	5. capless	8. tubes
3. wireless	6. spiteful	

merēly cāreless; completely blameless; a lonely spot

Pages 85-87 – Practice

Page 88

Vocabulary in these groups is not quite as difficult as in Level I. Good practice in categorizing.

KEY:

TT 2. rice; 3. Kate; 4. mules; 5. bike; 6. plugs; 7. like; 8. fuse; 9.race; 10. snore;
1. plume; 12. cake; 13. mops; 14. gallon. Pictures: spoon.

Page 89

KEY:

TT 2. rote; 3. dill; 4. kids; 5. rest; 6. putts; 7. strict; 8. stone; 9. tame; 10. wine;
11. snake; 12. stacks; 13. bend; 14. mutt. Pictures: flower.

Note: The following vowel-consonant-<u>e</u> <u>irregular</u> words are common and should be learned by Techniques 4 and 5 for reading and spelling: come, some, are, have, give, one. Other common irregular words with this pattern are: done, eye, gone, live, lose, love, move, none, prove, sure, there, were, where, whole, whose.

Level III

Level III tests for reading and spelling are located in the Appendix for evaluation purposes.

Sample behavioral objectives for Level III:

Upon the completion of Level III for reading training:

1. When presented with the vowel-r reading cards (ar, er, ir, or, wor, ur), the student will be able to respond orally with the key word and sound of the phonograms, (including the unaccented second sounds of ar and or) for each card with 100 percent accuracy.

2. When presented with the reading card g, the student will be able to respond with the additional (j) sound and the conditions for its use with 100 percent accuracy.

3. The student, when presented with the consonant digraph or trigraph dge, sh, ch, tch, th, wh, and ph, will be able to respond with the key words and sounds for each phonogram with 100 percent accuracy.

4. When presented with the 15 words listed in Test III-A containing only phonograms and concepts presented in Levels I and II plus vowel-r (presented in Level III), the student will read the list orally with 80 percent accuracy.

5. When presented with Test III-B, containing 20 words with the letter g in various situations, the student will be able to read the list orally with 80 percent accuracy.

6. When presented with Test III-C, containing 10 words with the consonant digraphs and trigraph sh, ch, and tch, the student will read the list with 90 percent accuracy.

7. When presented with Test III-D, containing 10 words with the consonant digraphs th, wh, and ph, the student will read the list orally with 80 percent accuracy.

8. When presented the Test III-E, containing 10 words with the -es suffix, the student will be able to read the list orally with 80 percent accuracy.

Upon completion of Level III for spelling training:

1. The student, when presented with the sounds (ûr), (är), (ôr), (th), (th̶), (wh), and (sh), will be able to respond with the regular letter spelling for each sound with 100 percent accuracy.

2. The student, when writing from dictation the 8 words of Test III-1, which contain only phonograms and concepts introduced in Levels I and II and er, or, and ar in regular pattern, will be able to spell correctly at least 6 of the words.

3. The student, when presented with the sound (j), will be able to respond with

TT   the four possible spellings (j, g, dge, ge) and conditions and demonstrate his understanding of their use by writing from dictation the 10 words of Test III-2, which illustrate this generalization, with 80 percent accuracy.

4. The student, when presented with the (ch) sound, will be able to respond with

TT   the spelling ch and tch and demonstrate his understanding of the (ch) spelling generalization by writing from dictation the 8 words of Test III-3, which illustrate this generalization, correctly spelling at least 6 words.

5. When presented with the dictation of the 10 words in Test III-4, which contain consonant digraphs and the -es suffix, the student will be able to write the correct spelling of at least 8 words.

Pages 90-92

1. A careful reading of these summary pages reveals that Level III concentrates on the vowel-r situations, the soft g (j), and consonant digraphs.

2. The preparation at the top of 90 reviews the V r r V pattern, which retains the short vowel sound, and the vowel-r e words with a slightly modified long vowel sound.

3. The main concept to be developed in the first pages of Level III is that the sound of a vowel before an r is altered by the r but only at the end of a word or when any consonant except another r follows the r. Consequently, if a *vowel* follows the vowel-r, the first vowel sound is not changed by the r but follows the regular patterns of pronunciation of open or closed syllables, (examples: merit, very.)

Page 93

1. Introduce for reading, er - fern (ûr); the sound picture in accented syllables is ûr). The sound picture for unaccented er is properly written (ẽr), but both have the same pronunciation. An er is regularly read (ûr) at the end of a word or before any consonant except another r.

2. This phonogram usually gives little problem to students, and many of these words are already familiar.

Page 94

1. Emphasize the concept of the suffix -er meaning "one who" or "that which" by drill in column 3 with statements like, "A banker is one who banks," etc.

2. The comparative suffix -er meaning "more than" when comparing two items, is often already familiar to many students. Emphasize that one horse is faster, or "more fast than" another.

3. Spelling: er is considered the regular spelling for the (ûr) sound since it is the most frequently used. All the other vowels in combination with r can also be pronounced (ûr) in certain situations, but these spellings are considered irregular and must be learned.

4. Add the spelling card: (ûr) with the response e r.

Page 95

1. This page reviews visually the concept of the r controlled e and tests it with
TT   nonsense words. This approach is sometimes beyond the understanding of the less-able student.

2. Students read the nonsense groups as vertical trios. No examples are given
TT   here of the V-r-V pattern because it is not covered until Level IV.

3. Do not use WORKBOOK – *page 33* until after 98 of the Study Book.

Page 96

1. Introduce the reading card ur – turtle (ûr). It is regular and easy for most students, especially since urr has the same sound.

2. Ur is irregular for spelling.

Page 97

1. Add ir (ûr). It appears in a limited number of words and is therefore difficult for many students to remember. Key word is bird.

2. Ir is irregular for spelling.

Page 98

1. This page reviews the ir situations as page 95 did with er. Do not spend excessive time on this page if it is difficult.

2. Note the exception of the familiar word <u>squirrel</u>.

3. WORKBOOK – *page 33* – Mark as on Study Book pages 95 and 98.

Page 99

1. Introduce <u>or</u> – <u>fork</u> (ôr), regular in an accented syllable at the end of a word (<u>for</u>) or before any consonant except another <u>r</u> (<u>fork</u>).

2. <u>Or</u> is regular for spelling (ôr) in a base word (examples above). Add the spelling card (ôr), response (ôr) <u>o</u> <u>r</u>.

Page 100

1. Add <u>or</u> – <u>doctor</u> (ẽr), regular for reading in a final unaccented syllable. Note that this syllable can either be part of the base word or the suffix meaning "one who" or "that which"; an <u>actor</u> is one who acts.

2. Remember that <u>or</u> is not the regular choice for spelling the suffix pronounced (ẽr); <u>er</u> is.

3. Add the reading card <u>wor</u> – <u>worm</u> (wûr), regular for reading. The letter *w* is again influencing the vowel sound *following* it.

4. <u>Wor</u> is regular for spelling the (wûr) sound at the beginning of a word. Add the response to the spelling card: (ûr) – <u>er</u>, after (w) – <u>or</u>.

5. Spelling:

1. form	4. berry	7. pester	10. orbit
2. limber	5. hanger	8. ornate	11. rafter
3. stork	6. corn	9. welder	12. hermit

6. WORKBOOK – *page 93* – recognizing the suffix -<u>er</u>, -<u>or</u>.

TT KEY:

Words with the suffixes circled: banker, hanger, killer, printer, surfer, renter, welder, drifter, duller, bumper, curler, lesser, passer, blocker, buffer, sifter, picker, kicker;

instructor, investor, actor, conductor, inventor, confessor, objector, collector.

Page 101

Review of the *or* situation for reading. Note that the <u>ore</u> in <u>sore</u> is very close in sound to <u>fôr</u> and may cause some difficulties in spelling. Remember the short <u>o</u> before <u>r</u> <u>r</u>.

1. Introduce <u>ar</u> – <u>star</u> (är), regular for reading and spelling in an accented syllable at the end of a word and before consonants except <u>r</u>. Remember that the double <u>rr</u> causes the <u>a</u> to retain its short sound, as in <u>marry</u>.

2. Spelling: Add the (är) card – response <u>a r</u>.

1. bark	4. stark	7. cord	10. market
2. spar	5. mart	8. carpet	
3. yard	6. harvest	9. absorb	

   a cork for the jar; the worst wart; orlon yarn.

1. Add the unaccented <u>ar</u>, (ēr) in a final unaccented syllable. Response to the reading card <u>ar</u> becomes: <u>star</u> (är), <u>dollar</u> (ēr).

2. Note that words in column two all have an <u>ard</u> final syllable which is not a true suffix. At the top of column three is the suffix -<u>ward</u>, meaning "direction toward; tendency to."

3. The <u>ar</u> becomes (ôr) after <u>w</u>. This <u>ar</u> spelling is regular for (ôr) after a <u>w</u>, (<u>wart</u>), or <u>qu</u>, (<u>quart</u>) but is not given as a response.

TT 1. Review check of the <u>ar</u> situation by nonsense words.

    2. WORKBOOK – *page 34* – Practice in marking vowels as on page 104.

    3. WORKBOOK – *page 35*

TT   KEY:
    1. mart, Target; 2. corral, sorrel; 3. denture; 4. expert, umpire; 5. errand, here; 6. tarry, herring; 7. person, Carrol.

    4. WORKBOOK – *page 36*

TT   KEY:
    star, stare, simmer, marry, scorn, sorry, horrid, sore, carton, carrot, canter, fire, party, pare, parrot, score;
    export, inquire, here, esquire, hire, word, bore, berry, rare, car, garlic, tire, wire, far, spare, worm.

Page 105

Students read these in vertical pairs – slowly if student has the tendency toward reversals.

Page 106

Good reading practice of mixed vowel-r words. Good review material for several lessons. Being able to read these words is good for students' confidence. Remind them that longer words are often easier to read than short because of familiar prefixes and suffixes and the fact that syllables follow rules for regularity more consistently than words do.

Page 107

Nonsense vowel-r words and sentences as a check of mastery.

Page 108-114

1. Reading practice to be used according to individual needs.

2. KEY to *page 111*: (Exercise involves vocabulary knowledge.) Matching to left column, in order: girl, back, care for, bunked in, dusty, sip, blink, song, mug.

3. Evaluation tests Level III-A for reading and III-1 for spelling found in Appendix can be given now as post-test.

Page 115

1. Introduce the second sound, (j), for g. Response to the g reading card becomes, "goat, (g), (j) before e, i, or y, usually." The word "usually" is included in the response and should be accented by the student. This pronunciation for g came from the French scribes after the Norman conquest. The exceptions for reading are largely of Germanic origin and include some common English words: get, gift, girl, give, giggle, gear, geese, geyser, gild, gill, gird, girdle, and girth.

2. WORKBOOK – *page 37* – For best results, this page should be done *before* reading page 115 of the Study Book for practice. This page concerns visually determining sound from spelling.
KEY:
Vertical column 1: gem (j), j, g, j, g, g, j, g;
2nd column: g, g, j, g, j, g, j, g, g.

3. The nonsense words in the first two columns of 115 are short and give good practice on the concept of the g controlled by a following e, i, or y. All ge, gi, or gy examples should be read with the (j).

4. The right columns of 115 should be read in horizontal pairs to illustrate the effect of adding the e to the g. In the bottom section, the addition of the e not only changes the (g) to (j) but also the short vowel sound to long.

TT

5. When the suffixes -ed, -y, and -ing are added to base words ending in g, the e, i, or y usually does *not* produce the change to a (j); thus the pronunciation of the base word remains identifiable: ringing, lagging, baggy, banged.

6. WORKBOOK – *page 38* – Translating the (j) into g or j from the visual clue of the following letter.

TT

KEY:
Top section, column 1: gene, jar, jog, gibe, gybe;
Col. 2: jab, gyp, jag, germ, jazz, joke;
Col. 3: jug, gin, gyre, jut, gem, jam;
Col. 4: gist, jade, gent, gym, junk, job.

Nonsense:
1st col.: giss, gemp, jaff, gile, gep, gesp, jub, jost;
2nd col.: gelk, juff, gisp, jact, geb, gyt, jast, gipe;
3rd col.: jull, gime, jope, gict, gine, juss, gend, jop.

Page 116

1. Practice in two and three-syllable words with g. In all of these, the g is pronounced (j) before e, i, or y.

2. WORKBOOK – *page 39*

   a. Student should copy the generalization at the top of the page into his notebook.

   b. Note the * is keyed to the * at the top of the page, for words with the root syllables ject. Some of these words are VCV words, which are presented as a pattern in Level IV, but the syllable division and accent are here marked and the student has already learned that open accented syllables are long.

   c. KEY:
   1st col.: Trojan, urgent, inject, Virgil, giblets, gypsy, digit, legend, interject, rigid, gentile;
   2nd col.: jasper, subject, suggest, magic, congest, logic, reject, junket, gender, conject, perjure, adjust;

64

3rd col.: wager, justin, ginger, margin, major, jolly, stingy, gesture, gypsum, German, merger, frigid.

Page 117

1. The top section is structured for the student to discover that the <u>dge</u> spelling of (j) immediately follows a short vowel sound and the <u>ge</u> follows a long vowel sound or a consonant. If the <u>d</u> was not in the <u>dge</u>, the pattern would be vowel-g-<u>e</u> and the vowel could not be short.

2. Add the <u>dge</u> card for reading: <u>badge</u> – (j).

3. The student should read the bottom left column horizontally. Changing the spelling of g to <u>dge</u> or <u>ge</u> of course changes the pronunciation to (j).

4. WORKBOOK – *page 40*

    a. This exercise concerns determining the spelling of final (j) from the visual clue of the letter preceding the (j). A short vowel immediately preceding the (j) in a one-syllable word demands a <u>dge</u>.

    b. KEY:
    Top: bulge-bulge.
    1st Col.: age, doge, cage, purge, dredge, cringe, huge, edge, fringe, gorge, fudge, indulge, hinge, grudge, large, lunge.
    2nd Col.: hedge, verge, lodge, page, plunge, ledge, singe, sage, midge, nudge, rage, pledge, splurge, ridge, sedge, stage;
    3rd Col.: sledge, rampage, urge, smudge, wedge, wage, trudge, tinge, bridge, drudge, submerge, forge, bilge, flange, stodge, gage.

5. Add <u>dge</u> and <u>ge</u> as responses to (j) for spelling. Response to (j) becomes: "j, g before <u>e</u>, <u>i</u>, or <u>y</u> usually; <u>ge</u> at the end; and <u>dge</u>."

Page 118

1. Emphasize that a final unaccented -<u>age</u> is pronounced (ĭj), not (āj) and watch for this error. The -<u>age</u> may be either the end of a base word or a suffix which means "a relationship with."

2. The regular spelling for (ĭj) at the end of a multisyllable word is -<u>age</u>.

3. WORKBOOK – *page 94* – To discriminate whether the letters before the -<u>age</u> form a base word which is connected in meaning with the given word.
    KEY:

AA Words that should have the -<u>age</u> circled: nestage, spillage, wordage, sinkage, driftage, wattage, linkage, stampage, swellage;

passage, blockage, mileage, yardage, windage, trackage, tillage, hermitage, percentage

4. WORKBOOK – *page 41*

    a. Students should copy the two parts of the generalization for (j) into notebook.

TT   b. Dictate these words in random order in the first section for students to determine whether to use g or j and to list in proper column on their papers:

       Under g: gent, gist, margin. Under j: junk, joke, jasper.

    c. Lower section: spelling the (j) at the end of a word. Dictate the following words in mixed order for the student to write in the correct column on his paper:

TT   Use <u>dge</u>: dodge, wedge, nudge, bridge.

       Use <u>ge</u>: sage, barge, plunge, huge.

       Use -<u>age</u>: baggage, bandage, village, advantage. (Remember about "rabbit" words!)

5. WORKBOOK – *page 42*

TT   KEY:

    1. hedge, edge, ledge, large. 2. hug, huge. 3. judge, grudge, pledge, dodge, charge. 4. budge, bulge, bridge. 5. wag, wage. 6. rag, rage. 7. Marge, village, rummage.

Page 119

1. Add the cards for the digraph <u>sh</u> – <u>ship</u> (sh); regular for reading and spelling. A digraph is composed of two letters pronounced with one sound.

2. Watch for confusions with (s) or (ch) on the part of some students with auditory confusions and prepare discrimination drills if these persist.

Page 120

1. Delay doing WORKBOOK – *page 64* before this page until all the consonant digraphs covered on it have been introduced (page 126).

2. Note the suffix -<u>ish</u> meaning "somewhat" in <u>pinkish</u>, "characteristic of" in <u>girlish</u>, and "belonging to" in <u>Turkish</u>. The suffix -<u>ship</u> is added to nouns to make other nouns and means "the quality or state of" or "the rank of."

3. Note that the digraphs are treated as one consonant in syllable division: mar/shal, not mars/hal.

4. Spelling:

1. page	4. edge	7. dashing	10. shrub
2. budge	5. tarnish	8. shock	11. sunshine
3. bondage	6. shine	9. shed	12. hardship

shuck the corn; ship his luggage; a rash from shell fish.

Pages 121-22

1. Introduce <u>ch</u> – <u>chair</u> (ch), a digraph regular for reading and spelling. Add both cards; all responses are applicable after page 124. Watch for confusion between *ch* and *sh* or with the voiced partner (j).

2. Spelling:

1. chum	4. chose	7. torch	10. charge
2. check	5. march	8. chapter	
3. brunch	6. champ	9. archer	

Page 123

1. Introduce these two pronunciations of <u>ch</u> but stress that these words come from two other languages and this explains these two sounds for <u>ch</u>. (ch) is the regular English pronunciation.

2. <u>Ch</u> as (k) is regular for words from the Greek language; most of these words are scientific, medical, or technical. Most of column 2 can be skipped if desired.

3. The <u>ch</u> pronounced (sh) is found in French words. The words listed in column three are the most common of these words and should be read through for familiarity. There are not many common (sh) pronunciations for <u>ch</u> in most vocabularies.

4. The two responses, Christmas (k); chef (sh), may be omitted for the reading card <u>ch</u> on the Skills Level. When presented with an unfamiliar word containing <u>ch</u>, the student should always try the (ch) English pronunciation first unless other letters in the word signal a Greek word (<u>ph</u>, <u>ism</u>, <u>mn</u>, <u>ps</u>, medial <u>y</u>); then the (k) would be logical.

Page 124

1. Introduce <u>tch</u> – <u>witch</u> (ch), a trigraph, regular for reading; add the card. Stress that the <u>t</u> is not pronounced but is a spelling inherited from Old English.

2. See if the students can discover visually from inspecting this page that tch is the spelling for (ch) used immediately after a short vowel and usually at the end of a monosyllable. Can they remember the two similar spelling situations (ck and dge)? Review pages 31 and 117 for reading and visual reinforcement of the spelling convention.

3. WORKBOOK – *page 43*

    a. The spelling generalization given at the top of 43 should be presented and copied here.

    b. The common words which, rich, much, and such are exceptions to this generalization which present no problem for reading but must be learned for spelling; sandwich is a multisyllable word so it would not apply.

    c. Dictation list to be given in mixed order and written by the student under correct columns on his paper, as on 41.

       Use ch: chip, chime, munch, filch, quench, march, lunch, chick, charter, ranch, punch.

       Use tch: pitch, notch, itch, blotch, stretch, match, watch, Dutch, latch, witch, sketch.

4. WORKBOOK – *page 44* – Spelling (ch) from the visual clue of the preceding letter. Note that in the top sections the words are paired horizontally to stress the concept.

TT   KEY:

    1st col.: March, hunch, crutch, witch, batch, bench, catch, clutch, ditch, Dutch, branch, church, etch, clinch, quench, hitch;

    2nd col.: match, hutch, crunch, winch, French, notch, blanch, lunch, fetch, splotch, munch, torch, bunch, swatch*, cratch, cinch;

    3rd col.: pitch, patch, finch, scorch, flinch, hatch, filch, sketch, scratch, snatch, stretch, trench, blotch, mulch, stench, squelch, twitch;

    4th col.: pinch, parch, fitch, Scotch, flitch, latch, watch*, brunch, lurch, punch, hotch, starch, botch, switch, stitch, ranch, ketch.

    * The wa follows the generalization even though the w influences the short sound of a.

5. The spelling response to (ch) is now ch and tch.

Page 125

Add th – thimble (th) to the reading cards; it is the unvoiced pronunciation of th.

68

1. WORKBOOK – *page 64*

    a. The bottom section of page 64 should be done *before* 126 of the Study Book. The concept to be emphasized is that the letters in consonant digraphs stick together and are treated as one consonant.

    b. KEY: (to bottom section)
    <u>sh</u>: fre<u>sh</u>/man, mar/<u>sh</u>al, ca<u>sh</u>/mere, wor/<u>sh</u>ip;
    <u>ch</u>: mer/<u>ch</u>ant, en/<u>ch</u>ant, or/<u>ch</u>ard, fran/<u>ch</u>ise, pen/<u>ch</u>ant;
    <u>th</u>: pan/<u>th</u>er, e<u>th</u>/nic, men/<u>th</u>ol, Ar/<u>th</u>ur, Ka<u>th</u>/ryn.

2. In the second column, the voiced <u>th</u> (th) is introduced. The reading card response becomes "<u>th</u>imble (th), <u>that</u> (t̶h̶)."

3. <u>Th</u> is the regular spelling for both sounds, (th) and (t̶h̶). Add the spelling cards.

4. At the bottom of the third column, attention is called to the pattern of a final <u>e</u> added to a <u>th</u> changing the vowel to long, as in the v-con-<u>e</u>, and the unvoiced <u>th</u> to (t̶h̶). Read across.

1. Introduce the reading card <u>wh</u> (hw) with the key word <u>whistle</u>. The <u>wh</u> pronunciation is made by blowing out air, as in the (h) with the (w) lip position. Demonstrate by having the student hold his hand in front of his mouth and say <u>will</u> and then <u>whip</u> and feel his breath on his hand with <u>whip</u>.

2. <u>Wh</u> is rarely at the end of an English base word. It is termed a "combination," not a digraph, since it is two sounds blended together in reverse order from the spelling. The <u>hw</u> order of pronunciation was the original spelling of many of the Old English words now spelled <u>wh</u> at the first of the word.

3. In certain parts of the United States <u>w</u> and <u>wh</u> are pronounced identically; some students also cannot discriminate auditorily between them. In such cases practice should not be allowed to become frustrating. The words at the top of page 127 are arranged in horizontal pairs to emphasize this discrimination.

4. Common exceptions to <u>wh</u> pronounced (hw) are the silent <u>w</u> in <u>who, whose, whom, whole, whooping</u>, etc. These are from Anglo-Saxon and Middle English origin.

5. <u>Wh</u> is the regular spelling for (hw) and should be added as a spelling card and response.

6. Spelling:

1. whip	4. why	7. those	10. farther
2. whale	5. wish	8. bath	11. panther
3. west	6. when	9. thick	12. then

Page 128-29

1. These sentences make excellent practice for <u>wh</u> words.

2. Be sure the irregular words listed (<u>where, there, to, do, of</u>) are known for both reading and spelling.

Page 130

1. Add the reading card for <u>ph</u> – phone (f), regular for reading and found in words used in medicine, science, and scholastic works from the Greek language.

2. Practice on these lists may be limited for those students who will not be meeting this level of vocabulary in their education.

TT

3. WORKBOOK – *page 7* – Reviews <u>ff</u>, <u>ll</u>, <u>ss</u> rule, now including consonant digraphs. Unscrambling the letters is to emphasize the double letter position at the end of the word after a short vowel.

   KEY:
   1st col.: bass, spell, muss, skill, muff, cull, chill, whiff, brass, shell, dress, stuff, smell, shall, cliff, boss.
   2nd col.: swell, press, gruff, bless, quill, snuff, tress, thrill, bliss, quell, chaff, fess, skiff, twill, stress, chuff, shrill.

4. WORKBOOK – *page 45* – Unscramble exercise to emphasize final <u>ck</u>, <u>dge</u>, and <u>tch</u> immediately following a short vowel.

AA

   KEY:
   1st col.: fudge, block, bridge, shock, crutch, switch, brick, judge, wedge, scratch, stretch, pledge, hitch, drudge;
   2nd col.: budge, latch, witch, lodge, quick, hedge, patch, ridge, catch, chuck, fetch, notch, ledge, smudge, twitch, check, snatch.

5. The <u>ph</u> is not a regular spelling for (f) but should always be considered as the choice for (f) in spelling a scientific word.

1. This exercise can be approached as a puzzle. The student reads aloud what appear to be nonsense words, but with the regular pronunciation they become recognizable real words.

AA   KEY:

1st col.: golf, wish, while, buff, swish, felt, drift, bluff, fine, thrift, chime, ship, whisker, twelfth, gruff;

2nd col.: fix, mix, finch, whiff, fancy, flag, flip, frisky, suffix, sniff, suffer, cliff, elf, witch, ridge.

2. WORKBOOK – *page 32*

AA   KEY:

file, fill, French, thin, shelf, pith, whip, self, thrill, fetch, bridge, chin, chose, witch, fib;

whine, fun, puff, with, wide, his, fish, white, stiff, flat, chive, fig, filth, sixth, fifty.

1. The plural of words ending in <u>s</u>, <u>x</u>, <u>z</u>, <u>ch</u>, and <u>sh</u> is spelled -<u>es</u>, which forms a separate syllable so that it can be heard. Be sure the students understand the concept of "plural." Students should copy this spelling rule in the student notebook.

2. Students may read these lists horizontally to include one of each column in turn.

3. It is important to note the bottom section and have students practice these words for several lessons. They must recognize visually the base word ending in silent <u>e</u>, (which makes a v-con-<u>e</u> pattern in some words, signaling a long vowel sound), plus an <u>s</u>. Actually, the silent <u>e</u> has been dropped according to the forthcoming spelling rule and the <u>es</u> suffix added. Because of the sibilant sound of the final <u>ce</u>, <u>ge</u>, <u>se</u>, or <u>ze</u>, the <u>es</u> suffix must be pronounced as a separate syllable.

4. WORKBOOK – *page 112* – plurals.

KEY:

1st col.: lenses, lamps, glasses, shirts, axes, shrubs, fizzes, thrushes, snatches, rocks, paths, pacts, porches, passes, blasts, throngs, flecks;

2nd col.: stacks, flashes, riches, thrills, fixes, shucks, buzzes, wasps, fifths, churches, clashes, lengths, foxes, benches, trunks, flasks, splashes

3rd col.: necks, arches, blitzes, moths, mixes, whacks, berths, slushes, patches, hicks, waxes, stashes, specks, widths, jazzes, gashes, tenths;

4th col.: mosses, clicks, cinches, swishes, texts, boxes, ducts, whelps, twists, marshes, depths, swamps, gulches, myths, rashes, broths, clinches.

5. Additional spelling practice forming plurals of words ending in <u>s</u>, <u>x</u>, <u>z</u>, <u>ch</u>, and <u>sh</u> should be given.

Sample spelling drill: Ask the student to write the *plural* of the following dictated words:

1. an ant	4. a match	7. a hedge	10. a wage
2. a class	5. a rose	8. a mess	11. a dish
3. a stage	6. a torch	9. a box	12. a tax

Page 133-36

Practice reading with many -<u>es</u> suffixes and recently introduced phonograms. These couplets give practice in rhythmic reading.

Pages 137-38 – Spot the Odd

1. Student should read each four-word group aloud and make his choice of the word inappropriate in meaning.

2. This reading practice also involves fair vocabulary knowledge and practice

AA   in categorizing.

3. KEY: *page 137*
2. perches; 3. fixes; 4. watches; 5. sashes; 6. stitches; 7. itches; 8. trunks; 9. switches; 10. lurches; 11. slashes; 12. mashes; 13. charges; 14. surprises. Picture: ring.

AA 4. KEY: *page 138*
2. places; 3. ages; 4. curses; 5. glimpses; 6. braces; 7. judges; 8. quenches; 9. dances; 10. pages; 11. riches; 12. hunches; 13. graces; 14. losses.

Level IV

Level IV tests for reading and spelling are located in the Appendix for evaluation purposes.

Sample behavioral objectives for Level IV:

Upon the completion of Level IV:

1. When presented with 8 words in Test IV-A, which illustrate the V´/CV letter and accent pattern, the student will demonstrate his ability to read at least 6 of the words correctly.

2. When presented with the 8 words in Test IV-B, which illustrate the VC´/V pattern, the student will demonstrate his ability to read at least 6 of the words correctly.

3. When presented with the 8 words in Test IV-C, which are of either V´/CV or VC´/V pattern, the student will demonstrate his ability to read at least 6 of the words correctly, trying both pronunciations for any word he does not recognize orally with his first attempt.

4. When presented with the 14 words of Test IV-D, which illustrate the additional patterns of accent, vowel sounds, and consonant digraphs covered in Level IV, the student will demonstrate his ability to read at least 10 of the words correctly.

TT

5. Upon dictation of Test IV-1 list of 8 words in the VCV pattern which are regular for spelling, the student shall demonstrate his ability to write the correct spelling for at least 6 words.

Page 139

1. The teacher should study carefully the preparation and concepts to be developed in this important section before introducing it.

2. Note that Level IV deals with VCV patterns in which the syllable division and accent determine the pronunciation of the first vowel. The three basic patterns here, V´/CV (<u>pony</u>), VC´/V (<u>robin</u>), and V/CV´(<u>humane</u>), must be practiced enough to instill some understanding of this concept in the students. The variations in these patterns are grouped for visual reinforcement, and practice and can be used according to teacher discretion.

3. The spelling concepts listed here are important. Review the (s) spelling principle at the bottom of the page.

Page 140

1. Review auditory recognition of syllable and accent as introduced for page 16 of the Study Book. Can the student determine that the long vowel is at the end of an open accented syllable in la´zy, pu´pil, le´gal, si´lent, and o´ver?

2. Add the key word for the open accented long sound of each of the vowels in the reading stack. Responses become: a - apple (ă), apron (ā); e - edge (ĕ), even (ē); i - it (ĭ), pilot (ī); o - octopus (ŏ), open (ō); u - up (ŭ), unicorn (ū); (the responses to y have already been learned.)

3. Page 140 should be read in entirety and practiced until the concept of dividing the syllable after the long vowel is firmly established as the first choice in attacking an unknown VCV word.

4. Spelling: Student should copy in notebook: "A long vowel at the end of a syllable is spelled with the single vowel." Add the new response as the first for the long vowel sounds in the spelling card stack. Responses at this stage should be learned by rote and are: (ā) - a at the end of a syllable, a-consonant-e, (ē) - e at the end of a syllable, e-consonant-e; (ī) - i at the end of a syllable*, i-consonant-e, y at the end of a word (see drill from WORKBOOK, page 50, below); (ō) - o at the end of a syllable, o-consonant-e; (ū) - u at the end of a syllable, u-consonant-e.

   *Remember that y is not the regular spelling for (ī) except at the end of a word, even though it is regular for reading in the open accented position. Any word with y not in the end position must be learned as irregular, (hyphen).

5. Spelling:

1. fiber	4. student	7. latex	10. holy
2. gravy	5. even	8. tiger	11. climax
3. locate	6. open	9. stupid	12. motive

6. WORKBOOK – *page 50*

   a. Only (ī) can be used for this type of exercise at this point because the other long vowel sounds at the end employ vowel digraphs (Level V).

   b. This exercise involves spelling the long vowel sound in one of three ways determined by the *position* of the sound in the word. It strengthens the concept that a particular spelling of a vowel sound is the regular one in an open, closed, or final position in a word. The student may need to be drilled, "Is there only one consonant heard after the (ī) as in time? Then spell it i-con-e. Or is the (ī) at the end of a syllable with a whole syllable heard after it, like in fi/nal? Then i."

TT

74

c. The following words should be dictated in mixed order and written by the student in the proper one of three columns on his paper. (Such exercises may be done in parts over several lessons or shortened.)

1st col.: tidy, Irish migrate, tripod, tiny, fiber, ivy, spider;

2nd col.: strike, hike, spite, polite, unite, whine, deprive, fire;

3rd col.: fly, my, why, rely, sky, reply, satisfy, cry.

Page 141

1. While the first choice of syllable division in a VCV pattern is the V̄/CV practiced on 140, there are a number of words listed on 141 to prove that the VC´/V pattern is also common and should be tried as a second choice when the V´/CV pronunciation does not produce a recognizable word.

2. Students should read through all of this page in sections for daily practice, strengthening the concept of syllable division producing a closed accented syllable (VC´V), just as it did in Level I (VC´CV).

3. This pattern does not require a new response to the vowels in the reading pack since the short vowel in a closed syllable is already the learned short response (ap ple).

4. Note that in words like peril, cherub, parish, and lyric, (VrV pattern), the r acts like any other consonant and does not influence the preceding vowel due to a vowel's following it; the first vowel is short or long depending upon the syllable division. Review pages 95, 98, 101, and 104 to emphasize when the r does change the vowel sound.

5. VC´/V words are irregular for spelling and must be learned; the "rabbit" pattern words are more common and are considered regular.

Page 142

1. WORKBOOK – page 65

a. This page should be done *before* page 142 in the Study Book. It summarizes the concepts just established on pages 140-41.

1. A vowel at the end of an accented syllable is *long*: V´/CV

2. A vowel in a closed syllable is *short*: VC´/V

b. Divide the numbered pairs by visual clues. Then pronounce each possibility and check the correct one:

TT   1. prō/per, prŏp´/er; chā´/pel, chă´/pel; dō´/nate, dŏn´/ate.

75

c. Bottom exercise is practice in pronouncing the two possibilities without visual clues. The student writes the correct syllable division after pronunciation tries determine it for him.

TT   KEY:

clĭn´/ic, rĕl´/ish, vī´/rus, tō´/tal, drăg´/on, ā´/gent, ā´/corn, sŏl´/id, rū´/by, lī´/cense, dĕv´/il, fŏr´/est, tŏp´/ic, flā´/vor, mĕl´/lon, Pē´/ter, Vī´/king, cŏp´/y.

2. Page 142 contains the two patterns for VCV in mixed lists for oral drill.

3. The student should be reminded that in attacking unrecognized VCV pattern words, he first tries V´/CV, then VC´/V. If he does not recognize the word, he should be told which is the correct pronunciation of the two. All of this page should be covered in sections.

Page 143

1. WORKBOOK – *page 66* – to be done *before* page 143 of the Study Book; it covers three-syllable words with the two patterns.

KEY:

AA   1. rī´/văl/rў; 2. ĕn´/ẽr/gў; 2. lĭb´/ẽr/tў; 2. căl´/ĕn/dẽr; 1. vā´/căn/cў.
scav´/en/ger, prop´/er/ty, a´/gen/cy, pen´/al/ty;
tap´/es/try, gal´/ax/y, fre´/quen/cy, o´/ver/ture, ban´/is/ter;
cyl´/in/der, dy´/nas/ty, su´/per/vise, hem´/is/phere, reg´/is/ter.

2. Page 143 gives practice in three-syllable words employing these syllable division patterns. Emphasize the more familiar words.

3. <u>ch</u> is (k), <u>ch</u> is (sh).

4. Note that the first two columns have a closed second syllable, the third an open *accented* second syllable. Teacher or students should read four or five words at a time vertically to recognize the similarities in accent and vowel sound patterns.

Note: Since Level IV involves variations in the syllable division and accent patterns of VCV but contains no new phonograms, work may now be begun in Level V on 160, which begins with the more familiar vowel digraphs. Daily practice continues in Level IV also, providing variety in lessons and giving the student the feeling of progress.

Page 144

1. Introduce the pattern of V/CV´, showing that an <u>e</u>, <u>o</u>, or <u>u</u> in an open first syllable becomes half-long when the accent is on the second syllable. The long

sound is simply held for a shorter length of time. In oral practice, work for a true half-long sound, not a (ə)! This is important to help the student remember the spelling.

2. WORKBOOK – *page 67* – Visual and kinesthetic reinforcement of the concepts being covered.

AA

KEY:

3. rĕ/sult´; 3. hū̇/mānĕ´; 3. dĕ/vōtĕ´; 3. ū̇/nīte´; 3. pȯ/līte´.

Page 145

Mixed lists of the three patterns with two-syllable words.

Page 146

1. WORKBOOK – *page 68* – Written practice in syllable division. This page is done *before* Study Book page 146.

AA

KEY:

3. ȯ/lym´/pic; 3. ū̇/ten´/sil; 1. cū´/cum/ber; ĕ/lec´/tric; 2. lĕg´/is/late.

2. Page 146 gives practice in oral reading of three-syllable words with a VC´/CV division between the first two syllables and the half-long unaccented sound in the second.

3. Student or teacher reads words in groups, emphasizing the rhythm of the words in this pattern. There are some interesting words for vocabulary enrichment on this page; discussion encourages interest in meaning as well as word attack and enlivens the lesson.

Page 147

1. WORKBOOK – *page 69*

   a. Use this exercise before page 147. Discuss the explanation about i and y at the top of the page, emphasizing that an *unaccented* open syllable ending in i or y is not half-long but short.

   b. KEY:

   3. dĭ/vīnĕ´; 3. cĭ/gär´; 3. dĕ/nȳ´; 1. ī´/vȳ; 2. cĭt´/ȳ.

2. Page 147 presents the situation that the unaccented i is short, not half-long as e, o, and u. Words are grouped under the symbol pattern and again should be read to emphasize the common rhythm and pronunciation patterns.

Page 148

1. Three-syllable words using unaccented i̠ in the patterns noted at the top of the page. Some of these words are familiar and should give the student confidence in reading longer words.

2. Stress the rhythm of accent again in oral reading of these.

Page 149

1. This page concerns the unaccented a̠ pronunciation. It is here marked (à) and is called the obscure a." It is read as (ŭ).

2. Add the obscure a̠ as the third response to the a̠ reading card; key word response is banana (à).

3. Some of these words are rare and should not demand prolonged attention.

4. The regular spelling for (ŭ) at the end of a word is a̠. Add it as a spelling response to the (ŭ) card; (ŭ) – (ŭ) – "u in an accented syllable, a̠ at the end of an unaccented syllable or a word."

5. Many people are careless and may pronounce the half-long e̠, o̠, or u̠ (ŭ). This makes spelling very difficult. If the teacher and students will use the exact half-long pronunciation in drills, it has some carry-over for spelling.

Page 150

1. WORKBOOK – page 70 is to be done *before* page 150.
   KEY:
   At the top: 1. long. 2. short. 3. half-long, short, obscure.
   Students should copy and learn these statements.

TT Center: 3. Jà/păn´; 3. sà/lūt¢´.

AA Bottom: Pronounce the three possibilities. Correct:
   căm´/ĕl, dăm´/ăge, blā´zēr; bā´/sĭn, răp´/ĭd, ă/līke´, pà/rādé´;
   lā´/dỹ, Lăt´/ĭn, flā´/võr, à/dŏpt´; cà/dĕt´, crā´/zy, căb´/ĭn, à/dōré´.

2. On page 150, students should practice all of the top section of fairly common words to establish the pattern of à/CV´ (bà/năn´/à).

3. Students should do the lists at the bottom of the page slowly enough to distinguish which of the a sounds they are using.

Page 151

1. WORKBOOK – *page 71* – to be done before 151.

AA KEY: 3. À/lăs´/kà; 3. mà/jĕs´/tĭc; 3. À/pŏl´/lō;

78

Căd´/ĭl/lăc; vȧ/nĭl´/lȧ; căl´/ĕn/dãr; cȧ/lȳp´/sō; ȧ/bŭn´/dănt;
lăv´/ĕn/dẽr; văl´/ĕn/tīnȩ; vŏl/cā´/nō; pĕn´/tȧ/gŏn; tẽr´/rȧ/pĭn; cĭn´/nȧ/mŏn.

2. Page 151 provides excellent practice with *a* in the various situations in three-syllable words.

3. WORKBOOK – *page 72*

   a. The dots in this exercise do *not* indicate the number of letters in the matching syllable.

   b. KEY:
   Left col.: agent, Irish, copy, delta, donate, radish;
   female, closet, iris, cola, pity, locate;
   nylon, planet, Cuba, humid, camel, solid.
   Right col.: amaze, polite, unite, cigar, July, Japan;
   elect, divorce, rely, parade, pretend, cadet;
   supreme, divine, romance, adore, canal, beyond.

Page 152

AA   Check on the application of the three pronunciation possibilities studied, using nonsense words. Good practice for the student able to have grasped the concept fully and without frustrations in shifting pronunciation. Skip this page if it appears frustrating.

Page 153

1. Two level practice in applying pronunciation principles and then recogniz-
AA   ing words with scrambled syllables.

2. KEY:

1st. col.: paragraph, volcano, torpedo, balcony, incubate, alphabet, ornamet, Apollo, accident, dictaphone, antelope, victory, instrument, bandana, cathedral, salary.

2nd col.: separate, Italy, sympathy, tomato, vanity, vitamin, melody, continent, banana, antenna, diplomat, superman, pentagon, unicorn, universe, compliment.

Page 154

1. WORKBOOK – *page 73* – Concept of consonant digraphs treated as single consonants in syllable division. This exercise is done *before* reading page

154.

AA KEY: (Requires vocabulary knowledge or teacher assistance):

2. both´/er; 1. go´/pher, 3. a/shore´;

hy´/<u>ph</u>en; a´/<u>ph</u>id; me<u>th</u>´/od; fa<u>th</u>´/om; du<u>ch</u>´/ess; si´/<u>ph</u>on; py´/<u>th</u>on; u<u>sh</u>´/er; <u>wh</u>e<u>th</u>´/er; tro<u>ph</u>y; ga<u>th</u>´/er.

2. This page provides good review for consonant digraphs as well as syllable division practice.

Page 155

1. Do WORKBOOK *page 74 before* reading page 155. Follow directions and explanations on blends.

AA KEY: sus/pense, pro/<u>gr</u>am, o/<u>kr</u>a, de/<u>scr</u>ibe, dis/<u>tr</u>ict; re/<u>pl</u>y, es/cape, vi/<u>br</u>ate, de/<u>str</u>uct, pro/<u>scr</u>ibe; hy/<u>dr</u>ant, se/<u>cr</u>et, ras/cal, re/<u>str</u>ict, con/<u>str</u>uct.

2. Page 155 gives good practice in dividing syllables with possible consonant blends.

3. Stress here that the first choice is dividing between the consonants and then treating the letters as a blend if a recognizable word was not formed.

Page 156

1. Read for the students the four example words, using first the (s) sound, and then the (z). Discuss the meanings and uses of the two different words formed by the two pronunciations. Review the meanings of *adverb, verb,* and *noun.*

2. Note the statements in mid-page. An <u>s</u> between two vowels is more often pronounced (z). This is evidenced in the "<u>nose</u> - (z)" reading card second response to <u>s</u> already learned. A (s) after a vowel, followed by an <u>e</u>, <u>i</u>, or <u>y</u> is regularly spelled <u>c</u>. (An <u>s</u> used in this position would usually have the (z) pronunciation). The response "<u>c</u> between a vowel and <u>e</u>, <u>i</u>, or <u>y</u>, to the (s) spelling card was added in Level II.

3. Read the pairs horizontally and note applications of the statements above.

Pages 157-59

1. Practice in the VCV patterns in sentences.

2. Teach the irregular words <u>one</u>, <u>two</u>, <u>too</u>, <u>you</u>, <u>your</u>, <u>there</u>, and <u>where</u> for reading and spelling if they are not already known. Use Techniques 4 and 5.

Level V

Level V tests for reading and spelling are located in the Appendix for evaluation purposes.

Sample behavioral objectives for Level V:

Upon the completion of Level V for reading training:

1. When presented with the 19 vowel digraph and diphthong reading cards presented in Level V, the student will be able to respond orally without hesitation with the key word or words and the sounds for each phonogram with 100 percent accuracy.

2. When presented with the 16 words in Test V-A, containing the regular pronunciations of the digraphs <u>ee</u>, <u>ea</u>, <u>oo</u>, <u>ai</u>, and <u>ay</u>, the student will be able to demonstrate his ability to read the list orally with 75 percent accuracy.

3. When presented with the 12 words of Test V-B, containing the digraphs and diphthongs <u>oa</u>, <u>oe</u>, <u>ou</u>, and <u>ow</u>, the student will be able to read orally at least 10 of the words correctly.

4. When presented with the 10 words of Test V-C, containing the digraphs and diphthongs <u>au</u>, <u>aw</u>, <u>oi</u>, and <u>oy</u>, the student will be able to read orally at least 8 of the words correctly.

5. When presented with the 15 words of Test V-D, containing the less common digraphs <u>ue</u>, <u>ie</u>, <u>ei</u>, <u>ey</u>, <u>eu</u>, <u>ew</u>, <u>ui</u>, and <u>ous</u>, the student will be able to read orally at least 12 of the words correctly.

Upon completion of Level V for spelling training:

1. Upon dictation of the long sounds of the five vowels, the student will be able to respond with the regular spelling for each long vowel sound in the open syllable, the closed long syllable sound, and the final position with 100 percent accuracy.

2. Upon dictation of the sounds (o͞o), (o͝o), (ou), (au), and (oi), the student will demonstrate his ability to respond with the regular spellings for each sound with 100 percent accuracy.

3. Upon dictation of the 15 words regular for spelling listed in Test V-1, containing digraphs and diphthongs covered in Level V, the student will demonstrate his ability to write at least 12 of the words correctly.

Pages 160-61

Read these pages for the concepts to be developed in Level V concerning vowel digraphs and diphthongs. A vowel digraph is a combination of two vowels in one syllable having only one sound; a diphthong is a blend of two vowels in one syllable (<u>oi</u>, <u>oy</u>, <u>ou</u>t, <u>c</u>ow).

Page 162

1. Add <u>ee</u> (ē) to the reading deck, key words "three feet - (ē)"; it is regular for reading except at the end of a few French words like <u>fiancée</u>.

2. Most students can read <u>ee</u> easily. The pairs at the end of the third column give discrimination practice between <u>ee</u> (ē) and <u>e</u> (ĕ).

Page 163

1. The left column of pairs presents discrimination practice and should be read horizontally.

2. WORKBOOK – *page 75* – Only the first section is here applicable, so this page can best be delayed until after *page 172*. Note, however, the statement at the top of *page 75*: A vowel digraph or diphthong must stick together in a syllable; however, its sound does not change in an open or closed syllable.

3. WORKBOOK – *page 48* – Introduces <u>ee</u> as the regular spelling for (ē) with a consonant sound in monosyllables, (<u>feet</u>), and <u>e</u>-con-<u>e</u> in multisyllables (<u>complete</u>). The exercise is in translating sound pictures into spelling words, using the stated generalization.
KEY:

AA Top section, Col. 1: speed, compete, convene, supreme, greed, concrete, creed;
Col 2: tweed, skeet, complete, sleet, steer, ampere, bleed.
Nonsense: treep, avere, indete, dreed, heen, antreme; alene, sneel, screet, antere, leet, olete.

4. WORKBOOK – *page 49*

a. Students should copy the generalization at the top.

b. Dictate the following words in mixed order. Students should write them in correct columns, as on page 50:

AA   <u>e</u>: fever, revise, evil, detest, meter, regret, debate.
<u>ee</u>: queen, bleed, keep, speed, sweep, meek, sheen.
<u>e-e</u>: compete, convene, obsolete, concrete, adhere, extreme, complete.
final <u>ee</u>: tree, glee, spree, yankee, trustee, jubilee, amputee.

5. Response to the spelling card (ē) now is: "e at the end of a syllable, e-con-e in a one-syllable word, ee at the end."

Page 164

Additional ee practice. Students displaying no difficulties need not read all of these lists. Point out that there are three pages of ee words, proving it a common digraph.

Pages 165-66

1. Introduce the reading card ea - easel (ē), the regular first choice for reading ea, but not regular for spelling. (ee is!)
2. In the 3rd column of 166, the list of VCV words shows ea as the second V in the pattern. Because a long sound automatically is accented, the syllable with the digraph gets the accent and the first e is half-long. This is a visual clue to accent.

Page 167

1. The less frequent sounds for ea on page 167, (compare this page in length with the 7 columns on the preceding pages) should not be introduced until the ea (ē) is secure.
2. The response to the reading card ea becomes easel (ē), head (ĕ). Steak (ā) can be included, but since the words in column 3 are usually familiar, this response is not necessary if the common words are known.
3. The (ĕ) sound for ea in one or two-syllable words is from the Anglo-Saxon. These words are predominately common, practical terms used in everyday living. Note that the digraph syllable gets the accent in the VCV pattern, even though it is short.
4. Other irregular pronunciations of ea before r are in learn, early, and heart.
5. The ea (ē) should always be tried first with unfamiliar words, then the (ĕ).
6. The ea is not the regular spelling for (ĕ) and these words must be learned for spelling purposes when needed.

Page 168

Introduce oo - moon (o͞o), the long sound, a regular pronunciation for reading as the three pages of words would indicate.

Page 169

1. Practice with visual discrimination between <u>oo</u>, <u>o</u>, and <u>o-e</u>. Read groups horizontally. Phrases and sentences provide good drill material.

2. The <u>oo</u> is the regular spelling for (o͞o), and the card should be added for the spelling response. Students should be alerted, however, that after <u>l</u>, <u>r</u>, <u>t</u>, and <u>s</u> the letter <u>u</u> is pronounced (o͞o) in long situations (<u>ruby</u>, <u>rule</u>), in many geographical areas, and this would be a possibility for spelling the (o͞o).

Page 170

Multisyllable words with <u>oo</u>.

Page 171

1. Add the short (o͝o) sound for <u>oo</u>, <u>book</u>. Response to the reading card becomes <u>moon</u> (o͞o), <u>book</u> (o͝o). This short sound can be considered regular also and is particularly common before <u>k</u>.

2. Students should read through the one-syllable (o͞o) words and note that the longer words are predominately compounds from the short words on the list.

3. A few irregular words for reading with <u>oo</u> must be learned: door, floor, flood, blood.

4. The <u>oo</u> is regular for spelling (o͞o), and the spelling card should be added.

5. Spelling:

1. mood	4. agree	7. moot	10. three
2. need	5. sheep	8. fleet	11. proof
3. shook	6. crook	9. textbook	12. creek

Page 172

1. Add <u>ai</u> (ā), regular for reading in a base word. Key word is <u>sail</u>.

2. The <u>ai</u> is not for regular for spelling (ā), and words spelled with it must be learned for spelling.

3. WORKBOOK – *page 75*

   a. Read carefully the explanation of vowel digraphs and diphthongs sticking together in syllables.

   b. Syllable division most commonly follows the vowel digraph, but the sound is not changed by either division.

c. KEY:

AA   ee: g<u>ee</u>/zer, fr<u>ee</u>/dom, t<u>ee</u>/ter, w<u>ee</u>/vil, p<u>ee</u>/wee, b<u>ee</u>/line;

ea: b<u>ea</u>/ver, p<u>ea</u>/cock, b<u>ea</u>/con, qu<u>ea</u>/sy, s<u>ea</u>/son, d<u>ea</u>/con, tr<u>ea</u>/son, m<u>ea</u>/ger, w<u>ea</u>/sel;

oo: b<u>oo</u>/by, g<u>oo</u>/ber, b<u>oo</u>/ty, d<u>oo</u>/ly, h<u>oo</u>/doo, b<u>oo</u>/hoo, b<u>oo</u>/tee, c<u>oo</u>/ly;

ai: d<u>ai</u>/sy, r<u>ai</u>/sin, r<u>ai</u>/ment, d<u>ai</u>/men, tr<u>ai</u>/tor, t<u>ai</u>/lor.

Page 173

1. Note that in the words in the VCV list, the <u>ai</u> (ā) is the accented syllable.

2. <u>Ain</u> in a final, unaccented syllable is pronounced (ĭn), <u>Britain</u>.

3. Common exceptions for reading are <u>said</u>, <u>plaid</u>, and <u>aisle</u>.

Page 174

1. Introduce <u>ay</u> - tr<u>ay</u> (ā), regular for reading, and at the end of a base word for spelling, (ā). Add the reading card and the last spelling response to (ā).

2. Remember that English words do not end in <u>i</u>; therefore the <u>y</u> spelling with <u>ay</u> is used at the ends of words. Associate the <u>ai</u> and <u>ay</u> as a related pair in sounding and spelling.

3. WORKBOOK – *page 47*

TT a. The student should copy the (ā) spelling generalization into his notebook.

    b. Response to the spelling card (ā) becomes, "<u>a</u> at the end of a syllable; <u>a</u>-consonant-e; <u>ay</u> at the end."

    c. Students should list the following words, dictated in mixed order, in the proper three columns on their papers:

<u>a</u>: lady, saber, gravy, vacate, April, navy, hatred, bacon.

<u>a-e</u>: page, wave, crate, plate, inhale, captivate, crave, behave.

<u>ay</u>: stay, bay, sway, decay, portray, relay, display, pray.

Page 175

1. Review of digraphs covered to date in pairs or trios for discrimination. Read horizontally.

1. queen	4. snoop	7. hook	10. clay
2. spray	5. tweed	8. weep	11. boom
3. booklet	6. fray	9. stood	12. bee

Page 176

1. Introduce <u>oa</u> - <u>boat</u> (ō) and add the reading card. It is regular for reading but not for spelling. The word <u>broad</u> is the only common exception.

2. Review concept of the half-long, unaccented open vowels in the VCV list.

Page 177

Review by horizontal pairs and trios for discrimination practice.

Page 178

1. Introduce the reading card for <u>oe</u> - <u>toe</u> (ō), which occurs infrequently as a digraph. If these words are read several times, the inclusion of this reading card is optional. <u>Shoe</u>, <u>canoe</u>, and <u>poem</u> are exceptions to the (ō) pronunciation.

2. Introduce <u>ou</u> - <u>ouch</u> (ou), regular for reading and spelling within a word. It is a diphthong because the two vowel sounds are blended in a single syllable; diphthongs behave as vowel digraphs. Add both the reading and spelling cards with the first responses.

3. This is a difficult phonogram for many students to remember and should get careful attention. There are a number of irregular pronunciations for <u>ou</u>, but first choice in an unknown word should always be (ou).

Page 179

Additional practice for <u>ou</u> (ou). Note that in the VCV words, the <u>ou</u> is in the accented syllable, making the unaccented <u>a</u> obscure.

Pages 180-81

1. For many students it is helpful to introduce page 181, the <u>ow</u> spelling for (ou), next for reading, before 180.

2. *Page 180* includes the French words in which <u>ou</u> is (o͞o). The response to the reading card <u>ou</u> now is: <u>ouch</u> (ou), <u>soup</u> (o͞o). Some of these words can be omitted because of their rarity if they are confusing. <u>You</u> is the common word from this group.

3. *Page 181* introduces the <u>ow</u> (ou) for reading, <u>cow</u>. This is the other diphthong spelling for (ou); add the reading card with the first response.

4. The <u>ow</u> spelling is regular at the end of a base word and before vowels, while <u>ou</u> is regular at the beginning or middle of a word. <u>Ow</u> is sometimes used before a final <u>n</u> or <u>l</u> within words or at the end of a syllable (<u>down</u>).

5. The response to the spelling card (ou) is <u>ou</u>, <u>ow</u>. The <u>u</u> and <u>w</u> are related letters for spelling as <u>i</u> and <u>y</u> are: (<u>ai-ay</u>, <u>ei-ey</u>, <u>oi-oy</u>, <u>ou-ow</u>, <u>au-aw</u>, <u>eu-ew</u>.)

6. Spelling:

1. stay	4. gloom	7. cloud	10. cows
2. plow	5. chow	8. brook	11. rooster
3. bound	6. free	9. scout	12. decay

Page 182

1. Introduce the second sound for <u>ow</u> - <u>snow</u> (ō). Response to the reading card <u>ow</u> is now: <u>cow</u> (ou), <u>snow</u> (ō).

2. Note that the <u>ow</u> (ō) is usually seen at the end of words.

3. In an unfamiliar word with <u>ow</u>, the student should first try (ou), then (ō).

4. Some students have been taught to consider <u>w</u> a vowel in a vowel digraph. This manual does not.

5. Introduce <u>ow</u> as regular for spelling the final (ō) sound in English words. Response to the (ō) spelling card becomes "<u>o</u> at the end of a syllable; <u>o</u>-consonant-<u>e</u>; <u>ow</u> at the end."

6. WORKBOOK – *page 51.*

TT   a. Students should copy the generalization in the spelling notebook

b. Dictate the following words in mixed order for students to list in the correct column on their papers:
<u>o</u>: donate, soda, Roman, clover, moment, robust, program, profile.
<u>o-e</u>: bore, spoke, dome, slope, quote, remote, stroke, throne.
<u>ow</u>: grow, throw, arrow, follow, borrow, mow, shallow, window.
(Remember "rabbit" word spellings!)

Page 183

Review discrimination practice with digraphs. Read across. Note that only the most common choice of pronunciation is to be used on this page.

Page 184-85

1. Introduce <u>au</u> - <u>auto</u> (au) or (ô). This is regular for both reading and spelling within a base word; add the cards.

2. Give ample time for practice and mastery. This digraph is particularly hard for some students to remember.

3. Watch for auditory discrimination difficulties with (ŏ) and prepare drills containing both if necessary.

Page 186

1. Add <u>aw</u> - <u>saw</u> (aw) or (ô). This is the other spelling for <u>au</u>, regular at the end of a word since English words do not usually end in <u>u</u>. Note its use inside words before the same letters (<u>n</u>, <u>l</u>) that <u>ow</u> is sometimes used.

2. Spelling card (au) or (ô) response is <u>au</u>; <u>aw</u>. Note that <u>aw</u> and <u>ow</u> are regular spellings within a word before a vowel: <u>drawer</u>, <u>coward</u>. English words tend not to have three vowels together, which would be the case if <u>au</u> or <u>ow</u> were used here.

3. Spelling:

1. August	4. greet	7. slaw	10. audit
2. shooting	5. straw	8. spray	
3. flaw	6. haunt	9. fraud	

AA

Page 187

Review of digraphs and diphthongs in horizontal groups.

Page 188

Practice phrases and sentences with (au) and (ou).

Pages 189-90

Introduce and add the reading card for the diphthong <u>oi</u> - <u>coil</u> (oi). This pairs with <u>oy</u> on 191 as <u>ai</u>-<u>ay</u> do. This is also a difficult phonogram for some students.

Page 191

1. Add <u>oy</u> - <u>boy</u> (oi). Note that it is seen primarily on the end of words where English would not use an <u>i</u>. It is also regular within a word when followed by a vowel: <u>loyal</u>, <u>voyage</u>.

2. These diphthongs are regular for spelling (oi), <u>oi</u> inside a word, <u>oy</u> at the end or before a vowel. Add the spelling card.

3. WORKBOOK – *page 55*

a. Visual drill to determine the correct spelling by noting the position of the sound.

b. KEY:

(ou): mouth, bow, how, scout, south, plow, slouch, chow, allow, sow, sprout, bounce, ounce, endow, oust, trout, brow.

(au): cause, haunt, law, straw, fraud, staunch, sauce, flaw, pause, launch, thaw, taunt, gauze, claw, jaw, laud, slaw.

(oi): boil, coy, foil, voice, joy, coin, annoy, loin, oil, enjoy, join, toy, hoist, coil, employ, soy, broil.

c. Students should read answers aloud for practice.

Page 192

Review of digraphs and diphthongs in horizontal groups.

Page 193

Nonsense poems for drill with digraphs and diphthongs. (AA)

Page 194

1. Introduce <u>ue</u> (ū) or (o͞o) in some geographical areas after <u>l</u>, <u>r</u>, <u>s</u>, or <u>t</u>. Response to the reading card is "<u>argue</u> (ū), <u>clue</u> (o͞o)."

2. The use of <u>ue</u> at the end as a spelling for (ū) is another example of a spelling convention because English does not usually end words with <u>u</u>. Response for the spelling card (ū) now becomes "<u>u</u> at the end of a syllable; <u>u</u>-consonant-<u>e</u> at the end of a word."

3. WORKBOOK – *page 52*

   a. Students copy the generalization for spelling (ū); <u>ue</u> is the regular spelling at the end of a word.

   b. Dictate the following words in mixed order for the student to put in the
   TT   correct column on his paper:

   <u>u</u>: human, Cuba, pupil, tuna, tulip, unite, duplex, unit.
   <u>u-e</u>: duke, fume, huge, fuse, dispute, refuse, substitute, altitude.
   <u>ue</u>: due, clue, argue, continue, subdue, fondue, value, hue.

4. WORKBOOK – *page 53* – Review on spelling the final long sounds from visual sound pictures.

   KEY:
   gee, crow, bay, bow, cue, sly, hay, fee, pry, mow, stray, relay, rescue;
   levee, arrow, betray, agree, essay, argue, defy, minnow, decay, relay, fescue, degree, deny.

5. WORKBOOK – *page 54* – Additional sound pictures.
KEY:
Top section: grow, gray, glee, why, due;
AA   mellow, referee, barbecue, holiday, magnify.

    Nonsense, 1st col.: splow, zay, stree, dwy, bue, clow, snay, sply, stee;
    2nd col.: osinee, cannow, elofy, olidue, culonay, peltow, quintue, pitinay, ponatee.

6. WORKBOOK – *page 8* – Review of the ff, ll, ss rule, exercise also including words with vowel digraphs.
TT KEY:
    (f): buff, spoof, beef, cliff, loaf, dwarf; elf, huff, proof, surf, reef, stuff; stiff, sniff, scarf, whiff, wharf, hoof; snuff, turf, woof, muff, gruff, coif.
    (l): spool, broil, reel, drool, chill, cool, cull, dill, curl, teal; steel, foul, hull, ill, oil, seal, peel, lull, creel, mill; quill, tool, smell, feel, wool, thrill, wail, pool, will, spoil; feel, rill, coil, wheel, trail, sail, fool, quail, toil, trill.

7. WORKBOOK – *page 20*
  a. Review of the generalization for final (k), using k after two vowels.
TT   Dictate the following words: sleek, cheek, spook, nook, creek, crook, brook, seek.
  b. The bottom section is advanced and demonstrates the need to add a k in order to maintain a (k) sound before a suffix beginning with e, i, or y.
    KEY:
    panicky, politicking, picnicker, colicky, frolicked, trafficker; shellacking, mimicking, lilacky, mimicked, panicked, politicked, trafficking.

8. WORKBOOK – *page 43*
  a. See the coverage for page 124 for the Study Book in this manual. Words that can now be included, if the drill is to be repeated, include: under ch: chow, speech, couch, launch, pouch.
  b. Review of the use of tch and ch. A vowel digraph cannot be followed by tch.

Pages 195-96

1. Introduce and add ie (ē) for reading; key word is priest. Practice thoroughly.
2. Go over ie (ī), pie. Most of these can be read easily. Note the words where the final y has been changed to i before ed. Some students tend to give the (ī) pronunciation first for ie because of familiarity with these words.

This response (ī) can be omitted for regular practice in most cases to avoid this.

3. WORKBOOK – *page 76* – Involves vocabulary knowledge beyond the level
AA   of some students.

KEY: astronaut, automat, dinosaur, chickadee, avenue, Milwaukee, calorie, financier, continue, embroider, autograph, trapezoid, tenderloin, tarpaulin, volunteer, referee.

Page 197-98

Note instructions at the bottom of 197 to read through, first leaving out the underlined words in order to get meaning; then read aloud as a tongue twister.

Page 199

1. Add the reading card for ei (ē) and (ā). This digraph comes from Middle English and the (ē) is the most common response. The (ā) pronunciation is most often used before n. Response is ceiling (ē), vein (ā). Neither is regular for spelling.

2. WORKBOOK – *page 46*
   a. Review of tch, dge, and ck used directly after a short vowel.
   b. KEY:

   (ch): grouch, clutch, pooch, bunch, couch, haunch, pouch, quench, scratch, ouch, mooch, brunch, vouch, stretch, slouch, switch, screech.

   (j): gouge, ridge, lounge, stooge, pledge, hinge, sage, scrooge, page, scrounge, ledge, gorge, beige, plunge, cringe, wedge, siege.

   (k): look, speak, check, meek, chunk, soak, thank, sleek, joke, crook, peek, peck, rook, leak, beak, cook, reek.

Page 200

1. Add ey - key (ē), regular for reading and almost always found at the end of base words. Two common irregular uses are eye and the (ā) pronunciation on page 207 in the Study Book.

2. Emphasize that ey is not a regular spelling. A number of students tend to use ey for y as a suffix or ending. This is the end spelling for ei, as noted earlier.

Page 201

1. Add eu - feud (ū). When a prefix from the Greek, it means "good" or "beautiful." Watch for other Greek language clues in a word with eu (ph, y, pn,

mn, rh). Eu is uncommon as a digraph in purely English words. It has the same sound as ue.

2. A number of the words on this page are obviously scientific or medical and fairly rare; practice may be limited.

Page 202

1. Add ew - few (ū). This is the partner for eu, with the w final spelling again.

2. However, despite several common words like few, the ew is not considered the regular spelling for final (ū); ue is.

Page 203-4

Practice, stressing digraphs, especially for (ū).

Page 205-6

Review groups for all digraphs introduced. To be read in horizontal groups. Better go slowly!

Page 207

1. The ui (o͞o) in fruit is not given as a reading response card. Practice should center on these most common words.

2. The ey (ā) pronunciation is also not given as a regular response because of its limited use. Read through these words for familiarity.

Page 208

The final ous (ŭs) is common but does not need to be given as a card response. It is often a suffix meaning "full of." Students should read column one and parts of the other columns.

Page 209

Students read through silently before trying to read this in poetic rhythm without "twisting the tongue."

Page 210

Excellent evaluation of mastery of vowel digraphs by using nonsense words. AA Success with this denotes real mastery. Note that directions call for the most common pronunciation.

Level VI

Level VI tests for reading and spelling are located in the Appendix for evaluation purposes.

Sample behavioral objectives for Level VI:

Upon the completion of Level VI for reading training:

1. When presented with the 10 words in Test VI-A, which contain the (au) pronunciation of a, "kind-old words," eigh and igh, the student will demonstrate his ability to read at least 8 of the words correctly.

2. When presented with the 10 words of Test VI-B, which contain the consonant-le ending, the student will read at least 8 of the words correctly.

3. When presented with the 10 words of Test VI-C, which contain adjacent vowels, the student will demonstrate his ability to read at least 7 of the words correctly.

4. When presented with the 10 words of Test VI-D, which end in -tion or -sion, the student will read 80 percent of the words correctly.

5. When presented with the 10 words of Test VI-E, which contain assorted suffixes or silent letters, the student will be able to read 8 of the words correctly.

6. When presented with the 10 words of Test VI-F, which contain exceptional pronunciations for v-consonant-e endings, (y) for i, and ti and ci final syllables, the student will be able to read 7 of the words correctly.

7. When presented with the complete set of reading cards, the student will be able to make all responses with 90 percent accuracy.

Upon completion of Level VI for spelling training:

1. Upon dictation of Test VI-1 list of 8 words ending in the consonant-l e, the student will demonstrate his ability to write the correct spelling for at least 6 words.

2. Upon dictation of the Test VI-2 list of 8 words ending in -tion or -sion (zhŭn), the student will be able to write correctly at least 6 of the words.

3. Upon dictation of the complete set of sounds listed on the spelling cards, the student will be able to make the proper responses and write the correct spellings for 80 percent of the responses for regular spellings.

Pages 211-12

Study the phonograms and patterns introduced in this level and the concepts to be developed. Note that the phonograms are of assorted types which do not fit into any one of the previous level patterns.

Page 213

1. Introduce the scribal o (ŭ) with the key word <u>onion</u> and add it as the third response to the reading card <u>o</u>.

2. Note that this sound of <u>o</u> is found predominately before an <u>n</u>, <u>m</u>, or <u>v</u>. Since an <u>o</u> often has the regular sounds (ŏ) and (ō) before these letters, the regular sound should be tried first in an unfamiliar word.

3. Students should read through the whole page for familiarity with this group; many are common words.

4. This spelling for (ŭ) must be learned and is not regular.

Page 214

1. Introduce the <u>al</u> combination with the <u>a</u> regularly pronounced (ô) or (au) in one-syllable words before <u>l</u>. Add <u>ball</u> (au) as the fourth response to the <u>a</u> reading card.

2. The lists in the center section are multisyllable words in which the <u>al</u> is given the (au) sound instead of the regular, more common (ă). Read through for familiarity.

3. The regular spelling for (aul) in one-syllable words is <u>al</u> (bald) or <u>all</u> at the end.

4. Add <u>a</u> as the third response to the spelling card (au). It is regularly spelled <u>a</u> before <u>l</u> *only* in one-syllable words.

Page 215

1. Add the <u>eigh</u> reading card, with the key word <u>eight</u> (ā). Students may be familiar with this word and able to see this combination of letters as a whole. The <u>gh</u> spelling was introduced by the French scribes for an Anglo-Saxon phoneme; the sound disappeared but the spelling was retained.

2. Add <u>igh</u> - <u>light</u> (ī). This phonogram has the same background as <u>eigh</u>.

3. WORKBOOK – *page 56*
   a. Practice in reading the regular nonsense words in the left columns and matching them with the correctly spelled word on the right.
   b. KEY:
AA   boxes on the left: 1st: 5, 7, 1, 6, 2, 3, 4; 2nd: 5, 7, 1, 6, 2, 3, 4; 3rd: 7, 5, 1, 4, 3, 2, 6;
right boxes: 1st: 5 4, 7, 1, 2, 3, 6; 2nd: 5, 1, 7, 2, 6, 4, 3; 3rd: 6, 5, 1, 4, 2, 3, 7

4. WORKBOOK – *page 57* – Important exercise for all students who are able to understand this concept. The important point being made is the <u>regular</u> spellings for long vowel sounds.

AA KEY:

1st col.: tale, made, mane, sale, plane, pale, pane, fare, pare, stare, hare, hale, sore, rode, lone, bore, cokes;

2nd col.: tow, row, flow, throw, slow, steel, reel, heel, peek, peel, leek, seem, deer, beet, reed, meet, way, nay.

Page 216

"Fun word" spellings for real words. Good practice for those students able to do it. Do this in several sessions. This exercise reinforces the most common pronunciation of a vowel digraph.

AA KEY:

1st col.: ache, near, thief, school, blade, date, white, brute, wheel, haste, fate, plays, broke, feet, you, state, grow, dry, rude, beach, fleet, late, site, week.

2nd col.: root, wound, low, pray, sake, small, soup, crow, seek, scrape, niece, fly, blue, treat, reed, beard, cape, vote, sway, shield, name, slope, phrase, snow.

3rd col.: meet, by, flow, leak, seat, spray, spry, blow, flew, new, seem, mate, brake, wage, pie, chew, leaf, stake, poke, great, stall, creep, ray, dome.

Page 217

1. This group, here called "kind-old" words, is composed of some common words in which an <u>i</u> or <u>o</u> takes the long sound in a one-syllable word, contrary to the closed syllable-short vowel pattern.

2. Notice that these words seem to fall into sub-groups as listed in columns, with <u>ind</u>, <u>ild</u>, <u>old</u>, <u>ost</u>, <u>oll</u>, and <u>olt</u> the most frequent combinations. In an unfamiliar word, however, the short <u>i</u> or <u>o</u> should be tried first.

3. This group is not given as a reading response to a drill card but should be read through until it can be done with ease and familiarity.

4. The group at the bottom of the page constitutes a situation in which an <u>a</u> is given the long sound when followed by <u>two</u> consonants and usually a silent <u>e</u>. Many of these words are familiar, and the two consonants are usually <u>ng</u> or <u>st</u>.

5. WORKBOOK – *page 58–* further reinforcement of alternative ways to spell words which have the same sound.

AA   a. Note that the left column words are to end in <u>ed</u>. This is a review of the <u>ed</u> spelling of (d) added to a base word. This is to back up the concept presented in the first level, "Is final (d) part of a base word, spelled <u>d</u>, or is it a suffix spelled <u>ed</u>?"

    b. KEY:

        left col.: rayed, grayed, stayed, frayed, lowed, rowed, mowed, bowed, towed, lowed, clawed, mooed.

        right col. base words: wade, side, tide, pride, hide, road, strode, bold, told, gold, fold, brood.

Pages 218-19

The consonant-<u>le</u> final stable syllable which sticks together and is never accented; <u>ble</u> (b´l).

1. The syllable -<u>ble</u>, -<u>dle</u>, etc. is an exception to the rule that every syllable must have a vowel sound. The final <u>e</u> is silent.

2. Note the hints on reading by covering the <u>ble</u>, etc., syllable and reading the first syllable.

3. In reading, if a vowel immediately precedes the <u>ble</u>, etc., syllable, it must be accented and therefore given the long sound. Only in -<u>ckle</u> words is the syllable division directly before the <u>le</u>, leaving the <u>ck</u> intact to close the short vowel syllable.

4. Add the reading card number 73. The response is (b´l), (d´l), (t´l) with no key words.

5. The <u>ble</u>, etc., pattern is regular for spelling and the spelling card should be added.

6. WORKBOOK – *page 59*

    a. The top section exercise is to translate into spelling the phonetic picture of words of this pattern.

AA b. KEY:

        left col. top: pebble, bugle, fable, straddle, fiddle, tattle, noble, staple.

        right col: raffle, gable, hobble, gobble, stable, stifle, griddle, cradle.

    c. The bottom exercise should be delayed until after page 224.

7. Spelling dictation:

1. nibble	4. gable	7. struggle	10. stall
2. mall	5. meddle	8. noble	11. rifle
3. kettle	6. bald	9. ramble	12. doodle

Page 220

Multisyllable words ending in -ble, -dle, etc.

Page 221

1. The words ending in the sound (k´l). Note the ck after a short vowel, the k after an n or r, and the few words ending in cle.

2. Note: -cle is the regular spelling, however, for final (k´l) in words of more than two syllables.

3. WORKBOOK – *page 60*

   KEY: 1. pickle; 2. trundle; 3. idle; 4. throttle; 5. quibble, trifle; 6. kettle; 7. noble; 8. foible; 9. brickle; 10. scrabble.

4. WORKBOOK – *page 95*

   a. This exercise fits logically here and emphasizes the differences between -fle as a base word ending and -ful the suffix.

   b. KEY:
   (top): Words in which the (fŭl) is a suffix:
   fitful, faithful, forceful, restful, skillful, fateful, useful, prideful, graceful.
   (bottom): 2. scornful, scuffle; 3. muffle, rifle; 4. raffle, sinful; 5. baffle, faithful; 6. trifle, stifle; 7. cheerful, sniffle.

Pages 222-23

1. Practice with words containing a silent consonant before the le, usually t, but sometimes c. Repeat until pronunciation is rapid.

2. Practice for auditory discrimination between consonant-le endings and similar el, al, ol, or il endings. Students should pronounce and hear the vowel before the l in these groups.

3. Paragraph at the bottom of 223 is excellent practice for -le words.

Page 224 – medial ck

1. These words should provide no difficulties for reading. The ck signals a short preceding vowel. The ck spelling is necessary to keep the (k) before e, i, or y.

2. WORKBOOK – *page 59* (bottom)

    a. The bottom section of words presents the generalization that a (k) imme-
diately after a short vowel in the middle of a word is spelled <u>ck</u> before <u>e</u>,
<u>i</u>, or <u>y</u>.

TT b. KEY:

    left column: buckle, freckle, tickle, heckle, trickle, chicken, flicker;

    right column: cracker, bucket, rocket, cricket, thicket, pocket, snicker.

Page 225

1. WORKBOOK – *page 77* – is presented *before* page 225.

    a. Students look down the pairs of vowels in the left columns; select which
form vowel digraphs and diphthongs. Check with Phono-Cards if needed.

    b. Other adjacent vowels must have syllable divisions between them.

    c. The vertical word pairs emphasize the difference visually and auditorily
and should be read aloud in pairs, calling attention to the two vowel
sounds in the "non-digraph" combinations.

2. Note that the words on 225 can only be divided into syllables in one way.

3. In the bottom group of words, adjacent vowels are in the first syllable and a
consonant nearly always introduces the final syllable.

Page 226

Words on this page have adjacent vowels in a medial or final syllable. Note the
choice of syllable division possible in the first syllable in some of the words,
explained by <u>Goliath</u>.

Page 227

1. WORKBOOK – *page 78* is done *before* 227. Practice is with similar pairs
where one divides between vowels and another contains a vowel digraph. It
is advised to try the more common vowel digraph sound first.

2. Note the accent patterns for the groups on 227.

3. Notice that some of these words are foreign and that some divide between a
prefix or suffix and the base word.

4. WORKBOOK – *page 96*

    a. This exercise reinforces the concept of a suffix beginning with a conso-
nant being added to a base word without change in spelling. This often
leads to what appears to be a doubled letter.

b. Notice the explanation about l's in the footnote.

c. KEY:

soonness, keenness, thinness, wanness, openness, wheelless, hill-less; joyfully, lawfully, normally, usefully, fully, dully, finally, mentally.

Page 228

1. Introduce and add the reading card for -tion - station (shŭn). This common ending must be seen as a unit. Words ending in it should be practiced enough for students to detect the rhythm patterns in the longer words.

2. The syllable *before* the -tion gets the primary accent; if the letter before -tion is a vowel, it ends an open accented syllable and is consequently long, with the exception of an i which remains short.

3. The bottom section contains words ending in ition mixed with others. Remember to accent the syllable before the -tion.

4. Add the spelling card for (shŭn), response: t i o n. This is considered the regular, most common spelling.

5. Spelling dictation:

1. motion	4. haggle	7. edition	10. rejection
2. fraction	5. auction	8. solution	11. devotion
3. contortion	6. inflation	9. stifle	12. munition

Page 229

1. Three-syllable -tion words for practice according to individual needs. Practice pronouncing by separate syllables.

2. The bottom section demonstrates that after an s the -tion is read (chŭn) for easier pronunciation.

Page 230

1. Three-syllable -tion words with a V/CV pattern.

2. The middle section contains a V/blend pattern.

3. In the bottom section, adjacent vowels divide.

Page 231

Four-syllable words. Notice that the primary accent remains on the syllable before -tion.

Page 232

1. The explanation at the top of the page points our important clues for pronunciation of longer words; the vowel before -tion regularly takes into its syllable the consonant before it.

2. Students should read the pronunciation in the parentheses aloud to detect the difference the point of syllable division makes.

Pages 233-35

1. Increasingly longer -tion words with varied accent patterns.

2. Students should note the ease with which these longer words can be read in syllables. Reading these pages usually increases student confidence. Remember to practice reading by separating syllables also.

3. Call attention to the accent marks in longer words which show the rhythm of accent in English.

Page 236

1. Introduce the reading card and the first response for -sion - mansion (shŭn), pointing out that the si is given the (sh) pronunciation just as the ti in -tion.

2. Again the accent is generally on the syllable just preceding the -sion. Notice that the syllable is closed; hence the (sh) for si.

3. The sion spelling of (shŭn) is irregular and must be memorized. More advanced students could study the complicated situations that determine the sion spelling. Note the ssion after most short vowels.

Page 237

1. Add explosion (zhŭn) as the second response to the reading card -sion.

2. Notice that, in the words on this page, immediately preceding the -sion is either a vowel or a root ending in r. Can the student discover that the voiced (zh) pronunciation may be given the s because it is difficult to say (sh) in this situation, just as the (z) pronunciation for s is used?

3. Emphasize that the vowel in the syllable preceding the -sion is long (except i) because it is an open, accented syllable. Continue to develop the concept of English as a language with some dependable patterns of pronunciation and spelling

4. Add the spelling card (zhŭn) - s i o n.

5. Give auditory discrimination drills for (shŭn) and (zhŭn). Ask the student to say t i o n after words in which he hears (shŭn) and s i o n for (zhŭn):

division	ablution	extraction
selection	profusion	collision
notation	adhesion	occasion
excursion	volition	ration

6. Spelling dictation:

1. vision	4. version	7. cohesion
2. invasion	5. disruption	8. nation
3. erosion	6. fusion	

Page 238

1. This page calls attention to a group of words ending in the common final syllables, -ent, -ence, -ant, -ance, -ancy, and -ency. Pronunciation is not difficult for these words, and this page gives information and practice which may prove useful in spelling them.

2. Students should practice reading as directed, exaggerating the short vowel sound in the final syllable to reinforce for spelling.

AA 3. Be sure the students grasp the connection in the second group of words of those words with a (j) before (ūnt), (ūns), or (ūnsi) being spelled with a g which must necessarily be followed by an e or y, not an a. Note the same principle for c before e, i, or y.

4. The regular spelling is cy for (sĭ) at the end of base words; also note the exceptions spelled ense and anse listed at the bottom of the page.

Page 239

TT 1. The explanation at the top of this page should be discussed, including the footnote. This is a good opportunity to call attention to differences in American and British pronunciations.

2. Students should read all of these words since many are familiar but may be mispronounced; note the pronunciation in light of the information presented.

3. Notice that the final (ĕr ĭ) spelling is regularly a r y.

Pages 240-41

1. These pages show visually the base word plus suffix structure and give valuable practice in shifting the accent when the suffix is added.

2. Students should follow directions, pronouncing the base word first, then "closing" the word by pronouncing it with the suffix added, noting the shift in accent. This auditory feedback should reinforce the concept of accent for those with auditory difficulties. These pages accomplish several objectives simultaneously.

TT (appears to left of item 2)

Pages 242-43

1. Practice in reading words with a silent consonant, here grouped and marked for visual reinforcement of the concept of silent letters.

2. Remind students that these silent letters were once pronounced in the original language the words came from; stress the concept of evolution in languages which leads to some of our spelling irregularities.

3. The initial gn was found in a number of early languages, with the final gn from French. The kn is from the Middle English; rh, mn, and ps are Greek, bt is Latin, and the initial gh is Dutch. Other silent letters derive from changes in pronunciation over the years without matching changes in spelling.

Page 244

1. These are groups of words with a deviant pronunciation, which fall into natural groups.

2. They should be read through for familiarity, but the sounds are not added as responses to reading cards.

Page 245

1. This page lists groups of words in which the vowel consonant-e pattern does not produce a long vowel sound. Note the i with the (ē) pronunciation.

2. Students should read these words as groups for recognition of them as exceptions.

Page 246

1. This page presents the sizable group of words in which t is pronounced (ch) before long u, especially the -ture words. This is not added as a reading card response.

2. The (choo) pronunciation for tu is an easier one for a long u sound after (t).

Page 247

1. This page deals with an i receiving an alternative consonant y pronunciation, (y), in final syllables.

AA (appears to left of item 1)

2. Words are listed in groups and should be so practiced, saying them both with the division after the _i_ and with the (y) pronunciation.

3. The spelling aid of (y) in a final syllable spelled _i_ is an advanced one and should not be added as a spelling response for (y). Do not allow this spelling to confuse students.

4. Note in the footnotes the _oy_ spelling before vowels and the consonant _y_ at the beginning of syllables.

Pages 248-50

1. These pages deal with the common situation of _ti_, _si_, and _ci_ pronounced (sh) when introducing final syllables. These words are frequently mispronounced or are difficult for students who have not studied the principle.

2. Note the two points about accent listed on 248 which were also discussed for -_tion_ and -_sion_.

3. Practice on these pages is best done in small sections over a number of lessons.

Page 251

1. Note that the group of words ending in _ciate_ or _tiate_ have a long _a_ final syllable and are verbs. The -_ate_ is a Latin suffix which produces a verb form.

2. The paragraph for reading practice is an excellent check on the application of pronunciations presented in preceding pages.

Page 252

1. Groups of words are presented in which _a_ and _i_ are long at the end of unaccented syllables. Attention is directed to the base or companion words.

2. Words of 3-or-more syllables in which the final _y_ in -_fy_ is long, although unaccented, are in the right column. The -_fy_ is a Latin suffix meaning "to make," the addition of which forms verbs.

Pages 253-54

These pages give practice in visual discrimination by presenting minimal pairs or groups of more difficult similar words for reading. These exercises again give opportunity to emphasize how much difference in meaning a single letter can make in a word and the need for careful reading.

Level VII

Level VII tests for reading and spelling are located in the Appendix for evaluation purposes.

Sample behavioral objectives for Level VII:

Upon the completion of Level VII for reading training:

1. When presented with the 10 words in Test VII-A, which are base words with suffixes the addition of which involved changes in spelling, the student will demonstrate the ability to read at least 8 of the words correctly.

2. When presented with the 8 words of Test VII-B, which are base words ending in y plus a suffix, the student will demonstrate the ability to read at least 6 of the words correctly.

Upon completion of Level VI for spelling training:

1. Upon dictation of the 10 words of Test VII-1, involving base words ending in silent-e with a suffix, the student will be able to write the correct spelling of at least 7 words. (AA)

2. Upon dictation of the 10 words of Test VII-2, involving the 1-1-1 rule for doubling a consonant before a suffix, the student will be able to write the correct spelling of at least 8 words. (TT)

3. Upon dictation of the 10 words of Test VII-3, involving base words ending in y plus a suffix and 2-1-1 words with suffixes, the student will be able to write the correct spelling of at least 7 words. (AA)

4. Upon dictation of the 10 words of Test VII-4, which are plurals of words ending in sibilants or y, the student will be able to spell at least 8 of the words correctly in writing.

5. Upon dictation of the 8 words of Test VII-5, which are plurals of words ending in f or o or irregular plurals, the student will demonstrate the ability to write the correct spelling for at least 6 of the words. (TT)

6. Upon dictation of the 8 words of Test VII-6, which are ei-ie words, the student will demonstrate the ability to write correctly the spelling of at least 6 words. (AA)

7. Upon dictation of the 10 phrases of Test VII-7, the student will demonstrate the ability to write the possessive form of the noun or pronoun in each phrase with 80 percent accuracy in spelling. (AA)

Pages 255-56

1. Read carefully the summary of the presentation of Level VII which focuses on spelling rules and is developed primarily with WORKBOOK exercises.

2. Stress the important concept under *Preparation,* reviewing recognition of a
TT   base word plus a suffix as opposed to a simple base word. This influences
      both pronunciation and spelling.

3. Notice that the *Procedures* stress that only a few exercises are given in the
   WORKBOOK for each rule and that much additional practice is necessary
   for mastery. Spelling workbooks that resemble *Angling for Words* in spelling
   presentation are available from Educators Publishing Services, Inc.,
   Cambridge, Massachusetts.

4. Be sure not to present exceptions to the rules until the rule is completely
   mastered.

5. The sequence of presentation for the spelling rules is carefully outlined with
   the concepts and page numbers, and the order is important. *Angling* deals
   with the four spelling rules involving suffixes, the prefixes, the plural rules,
   possessives, and the base word <u>ie-ei</u> situation. Read carefully the accompa-
   nying notes in this outline.

Page 257

1. The WORKBOOK pages 97-100 are to be covered *before* 257.

2. WORKBOOK – *page 97* – This page of rules deals with the silent <u>e</u> rule and
   its exceptions. The <u>e</u> is *not* dropped before a suffix beginning with a *consonant.*

   a. Students should copy only the first sentence in their notebooks until the
      exceptions are covered.

   b. Students should be able to reason the necessity for keeping the <u>e</u> before
      <u>a</u> and <u>o</u> after <u>c</u> and <u>g</u>. This page summarizes various aspects of the rule.

3. WORKBOOK – *page 98*
   KEY:
   hopeless, hoping, hopeful, hoped; caring, careful, careless, cared; nicely,
   niceness, nicest; using, useful, usable, user, useless; timeless, timing, timer,
   timely; squarely, squaring, squareness; scary, scaring, scared; sloping, slopy,
   slopeless; statement, stating, stately.

4. WORKBOOK – *page 99*
   KEY:
   Col. 1: famous, wisely, biting, flaky, blameful, blaring, nosy, curing, close-
         ly, dared;
   Col. 2: palish, icy, joking, latest, lonely, jivy, likeness, lifeless, lining, prud-
         ish;
   Col. 3: diving, fakeness, stony, griping, grading, hiking, fateful, hugest,

105

fadeless, niceness.

5. WORKBOOK – *page 100*

    a. This exercise stresses visually the concept of the base word and the added suffix. When a base word that ends in <u>e</u> adds an <u>ed</u> suffix, the first <u>e</u> is dropped according to the rule and the suffix <u>ed</u> is added. Students should be drilled to recognize this concept and procedure; they are *not* adding a <u>d</u>!

    b. KEY:

    Top: marble+ed, fable+s, shuffle+ed, tangle+s, smuggle+ed;

    1st col.: humbly, cuddly, idleness, purplish, ably, mumbles, gently;

    2nd col.: gentleness, crumbly, ruffled, rumples, simply, bundles, settled.

6. Return to page 257 in the Study Book for reading practice with the silent <u>e</u> plus suffix words. Note the warning about final <u>l</u> <u>e</u> <u>d</u>; it is usually the <u>l</u> <u>e</u> ending of a base word plus an added -<u>ed</u> suffix. Students should focus on the base word.

7. Practice on the exceptions to the silent <u>e</u> rule, which are described on WORKBOOK page 97, is found on WORKBOOK pages 101-2. When the

AA   application of the regular rule is automatic with the students, the exceptions should be copied in spelling notebooks and learned *before* these exercises are done. Memorize all underlined exception words in point 2.

8. WORKBOOK – *page 102*

AA KEY:

completable, changeable, sliceable, inflatable, chargeable, hugeous, pronounceable, desirable, advantageous, admirable; manageable, knowledgeable, assumable, exchangeable, replaceable, disputable, damageable, packageable, refusable, dodgeable.

9. WORKBOOK – *page 102*

AA KEY: (The reason is listed as col. 1, 2, or 3)

wholeness, 2; wholly, 3; wholesome, 2; solely, 2; duly, 3; truly, 3; truth, 3; ninth, 3; awesome, 2; awful, 3; rueful, 2; arguing, 1; argument, 3; amusement, 2; resemblance, 1.

Pages 258-60

1. Teach <u>who</u>, <u>whose</u>, <u>some</u>, and <u>were</u> for reading and spelling by Techniques 4 and 5 if the student does not know them.

2. Students should prepare to read couplets in smooth rhythm by reading through silently first.

Involves the 1-1-1 rule and silent <u>e</u> rule. The following pages should be done in the WORKBOOK *before* 261.

1. WORKBOOK – *page 103*
    a. Students should copy the 1-1-1 rule given at the top of the page into spelling notebooks and memorize. The 1-1-1 obviously stands for <u>one</u> syllable, <u>one</u> consonant, <u>one</u> vowel. Only if all three conditions are met in a base word is the final consonant doubled before a suffix beginning with a vowel. The concept of there being a *reason* for doubling an English consonant should be emphasized.
    b. Note the consonants never doubled: <u>h</u>, <u>j</u>, <u>k</u>, <u>v</u>, <u>w</u>, <u>x</u>, <u>y</u>.
    c. KEY:

TT   fitting, fitter, fitful, fitted, fitness, fittable;
dimmest, dimmed, dimly, dimmer, dimness, dimming;
sinful, sinned, sinless, sinner;
thinner, thinly, thinned, thinnish, thinness, thinnest, thinnable;
sunning, sunny, sunned, sunless;
fogged, fogless, foggy, fogging, fogger.

2. WORKBOOK – *page 104*
    KEY:
    1st col.: batting, bidder, brimless,clipping, snappy, melted, weeping, flatly, dotting, drummer, dripped;
    2nd col.: wilted, thumped, sobbing, shedding, peppy, flipped, gladly, stripped, sledding, taxed, slipping;
    3rd col.: rubbing, limped, ripping, skinned, scooter, stopping, ramming, slapped, blotter, fixing, spinner.

3. WORKBOOK – *page 105* – the spelling rules mixed.
    KEY:

AA   snapping, shaming, stripping, rooming, golfing, riding, griping, dripping, coiling;
flaking, moping, stabbing, striping, pouting, taxing, icing, fibbing, snoring;
melting, whaling, fleeing, sharing, spotting, pining, whining, lagging, tooting.

Nonsense: Marked:

Add: cumb, joil, yoit, geel; rell, bir, sork, woop, bax;

Dbl: zon, miz, plun; yar, gir, lig, moz;

Drop: bave, kide, yipe, jole; jule, mive, hode, fafe.

4. WORKBOOK – *page 106* – reverses the spelling procedure, moving back to the base word from the altered word.
   KEY:

AA   scare, scar, stare, star, spare, spar, bare, bar, bore, tar, par, glare, care, fare, dare, glare, mar;
      rate, rat, mat, mate, cute, cut, robe, fur, dole, gap, snipe, hat, scrap, rid, tile, shame, bide.

Page 261

Reading mixed words of the silent e and 1-1-1 patterns.

1. Have the students study and discuss the explanation at the top of the page. Would it confuse a listener as to meaning if this spelling were not used?
2. Students should read a word and then pronounce the base word.
3. WORKBOOK – *page 107*
   a. This page presents the rule for adding suffixes to base words having the final 1-1 pattern but more than one syllable.

AA   b. The doubling of the final single consonant after one vowel in multisyllables depends not only on the suffix beginning with a vowel but on the last syllable's being *accented*. This rule is especially difficult for students with difficulties in determining accent.
   c. KEY: (Consider columns as 1, 2, 3, 4; X appears in these columns with all others being checks:)
      orbit-3, 4; prohibit-3, 4; avoid-1, 4; regret+ful-2, 4; open-3, 4; demand-1, 4.
4. WORKBOOK – *page 108*
   KEY:

AA   omitted, submitting, remittance, commitment, emitting, galloped, remaining, expelled, propeller, repellent, compelling, impelled, marooned;
      detailed, occurring, recurrent, concurred, gardener, gossipy, preferring, referred, deferment, inferred, limited, developed, detained.

5. WORKBOOK – *page 109*
   a. Begin study of the final y spelling rule, here applied to suffixes. Students should copy the rule and the exceptions into spelling notebooks and memorize.

TT   b. KEY: carrier, carried, carrying, carriage; appliance, applied, applying; married, marriage, marrying; business, busying, busier, busyish, busiest;

multiplying, multiplier, multiplied; studying, studied, studious; hurrying, hurried; easier, easiness, easyish, easiest; worried; envying, envied.

6. WORKBOOK – *page 110*

KEY:

AA   1st col.: boyish, cried, spying, fried, payment, complying, displayed, clumsiness, carrier, decoyed, prayed, crispier, catchiness;

2nd col.: dressiest, convoyed, gloomily, denying, envious, grayed, destroyed, enviable, business, funniest, deployed, employer, fluffiness;

3rd col.: enjoyment, glorious, frayed, joyous, implied, jolliest; relayed, justifying, satisfied, grouchiness, deployment, stickiness, annoyed.

Pages 262-63

AA 1. Students should pronounce each base word and then the word formed by adding the suffix, which has an altered pronunciation.

2. The part of speech is often changed by the addition. Discuss the changes in meaning caused by the added suffix.

Page 264

1. Note carefully the explanation at the top of the page. Students should copy this in spelling notebooks and learn. The endings -<u>cle</u> and -<u>gle</u> change their spelling to -<u>cular</u> and -<u>gular</u> when forming adjectives.

2. KEY:

1st col.: desirability, legibility, nobility, probability, responsibility, reliability, ability; circle, single, rectangle, angle, muscle, triangle, particle;

2nd col.: stable, durable, eligible, feasible, visible, liable, flexible; spectacular, vehicular, oracular, quadrangular, ventricular, tubercular, corpuscular.

Additional WORKBOOK pages are to be done at this point:

1. WORKBOOK – *page 79* – prefixes

a. This exercise points out that adding a prefix to a base word does not change the base word spelling even when it creates a double consonant.

b. Stress that a prefix does change the *meaning* of a word.

c. KEY:

misspell, misshape, misuse, misstate, misstep, mismatch, disagree, dissatisfy;

dissimilar, disinfect, unnoticed, unnumbered, unable, unnamed, unnatural, uneven.

2. WORKBOOK – *page 80*

   a. This exercise demands that a given word be broken down and returned to the original spelling of the prefix, base word, and suffix. It tests ability to apply the spelling rules in reverse, reconstructing the base word and suffix.

   b. KEY:

   dis+qualify+ed; un+occupy+ed; mis+use+age; re+shuffle+ed; dis+able+ed; ample+y; re+marry+age; dis+agree+able+y; un+necessary+ly; continue+ous; mis+handle+ed; dis+robe+ed; un+deny+able+y.

Review and further study of plural rules should be undertaken here.

1. Review the s and es rules in the WORKBOOK pages 111 and 112 done in Level I and III.

2. WORKBOOK – *page 113* – applies the y spelling rule to plurals.
   KEY:

   1st col.: ladies, boys, puppies, relays, doilies, armies, cherries, grays, follies, joys, forties, stories, candies, trays;

   2nd col.: tragedies, memories, sprays, melodies, victories, essays, salaries, displays arteries, counties, qualities, convoys, remedies, injuries.

3. WORKBOOK – *page 114*
   KEY:

   1st col.: agonies, industries, babies, subways, berries, fairies, keys, alleys, allies, daisies, buys, galleys, accuracies, batteries, monkeys, chimneys, activities;

   2nd col.: allegories, apologies, viceroys, mercies, lackeys, balconies, jerseys, cities, canopies, charities, envoys, attorneys, bunnies, buggies, cavities, parleys, calamities;

   3rd col.: communities, turkeys, utilities, donkeys, felonies, jockeys, fifties, gullies, kidneys, gravies, inlays, ditties, economies, draperies, bodies, pulleys, duties.

Page 265

1. This last page reviews the y spelling rule situation as it affects reading of the words.

2. In the first two columns, students should read each word and name each

base word.

3. In the third column, the original base word and the base word plus suffixes should each be determined. (Example: fuss, fussy, fussiness)

Workbook pages 115-124 are additional plural and possessive rules. Explanations at the top of these pages should be sufficient for instruction and the rules should be added to student notebooks and memorized.

1. WORKBOOK – *page 115* – f, fe plurals rule

   a. The movement in recent decades has been toward the simpler plural spellings with the s after f or fe instead of the original ves spelling. The words listed here retain the ves plural form.

   b. KEY: (to top section)

   elves, selves, shelves, lives, wives, knives, wolves; thieves, leaves, beeves, sheaves, halves, calves, loaves.

   Bottom section: elves, roofs, wolves, calves; halves, loaves, shelves; sheaves, knives; lives, themselves, goofs, beeves, griefs.

2. WORKBOOK – *page 116* – f, fe practice

   TT   KEY:

   1st col.: knives, reefs, briefs, elves, dwarfs, fifes, selves, leaves, woofs, strifes, lives;

   2nd col.: muffs, tiffs, serfs, puffs, loaves, buffs, reliefs, thieves, wolves, griefs, beliefs;

   3rd col.: waifs, oafs, skiffs, wives, whiffs, scuffs, surfs, cutoffs, shelves, proofs, halves;

   4th col.: chefs, calves, chiefs, tariffs, turfs, sheafs, giraffes, gulfs, handkerchiefs, stuffs, coifs;

   Blanks: sheriffs, bailiffs, wives, thieves, safes; thieves, themselves, leaves, sniffs, mastiffs, handcuffs.

3. WORKBOOK – *page 117* – o – plural rule

   a. Memorize the words that must add es. Some other o words can either have s or es as their plural form, but it is simpler to concentrate on these which must have the es form and spell all others s.

   b. The second group of six words are not common and need not be memorized by most students.

   c. KEY:

   1. Embargoes; 2. Echoes; 3. Vetoes; 4. Torpedoes; 5. Heroes; 6. Potatoes, tomatoes.

111

Bottom: ponchos, rhinos, tomatoes, potatoes;
          photos, torpedos, ratios, heroes;
          echoes, torsos, vetoes, pueblos;
          jingos, rodeos, embargoes, torpedoes.

4. WORKBOOK – *page 118* – final o rule practice

TT KEY:

1. Embargoes, curios; 2. zeros, vetoes; 3. ponchos, rodeos; 4. torpedoes, infernos, echoes; 5. Mosquitos, armadillos, hippos, rhinos; 6. Pianos, cellos, piccolos; 7. Burros, tomatoes; 8. Silos, potatoes, portfolios, mementos; 9. radios, patios, studios, heroes.

5. WORKBOOK – *page 119* – irregular plurals

    a. With the movement toward regular s or es plurals, only these few common words retain the original plural form without an s.

    b. Note that some change the vowels for the plural, some add letters or change them, and some keep the singular form for the plural.

    c. KEY:

    oxen, mice, feet, teeth, geese, lice, children, men, policemen, women, gentlemen, deer, sheep, moose, grouse, swine.

    1. o's, a's; 2. t's, i's; 3. t's; 4. V's, x's; 5. n's, u's; 6. +'s, -'s, x's, ÷'s, 7. 21's, 12's.

6. WORKBOOK – *page 120* – plurals review

    KEY:

    1st: mosses, altos, wolves, poppies, policemen, teeth, tubs, splashes, cows, parties, solos, decoys, knives, vetoes, woofs, elves, turkeys, fixes, pansies, snacks, rhinos, children;

    2nd: counties, patios, shelves, women, donkeys, heroes, chiefs, moths, gentlemen, deer, potatoes, relays, selves, plurals, rodeos, skies, waltzes, crutches, maps, torpedoes, companies, leaves;

    3rd: sheep, alleys, lullabies, pianos, kinsmen, chefs, rocks, wives, affixes, zoos, blitzes, tomatoes, dwarfs, laboratories, loaves, monkeys, racks, halves, geese, dittos, clefs, shampoos;

    4th: stacks, injuries, proofs, ashes, echoes, libraries, lives, swine, accents, envoys, thieves, feet, salaries, oxen, saws, studios, clashes, embargoes, gypsies, photos, men, rashes.

7. WORKBOOK – *page 121* – possessives rule

    a. Some students have confusions between plurals and possessives (because of the s) or between contractions and possessives (because of the apostrophe.) For those who have difficulty with the concept of singular and plural, the more simplified, newer possessive form may be taught, (Mr. Jones').

b. In this new approach to forming possessives, write the word which is the owner, lift the pencil, add the apostrophe to show possession, and then add s *only* if the original word did not end in s.

c. KEY:

Dogs, dog's; cat's, cats; Boys, boy's; store's, stores; fiddle's, autos', Ann's, tires', trees', zebra's, face's, windows', tables', shrub's.

8. WORKBOOK – *page 122*
KEY:

AA   doctor's, doctors, doctors'; policeman's, policemen, policemen's; baby's, babies, babies'; mouse's, mice, mice's; loaf's, loaves, loaves'; bird's, birds, birds'; ox's, oxen, oxen's; sheep's, sheep, sheep's.

1st: boys' PP, PP, SP, SP-PP, PP, SP, SP, SP, PP, PP, PP;

2nd: PP, SP-PP, PP, SP, SP-PP, SP, SP, PP, PP, PP, PP;

3rd: SP, PP, PP, SP, SP-PP, PP, SP, PP, SP, SP, PP

9. WORKBOOK – *page 123*
KEY:

AA   boy's, girls'; story's, stories', topaz's, elf's, companies', cats', ours, stamp's, clubs', witch's, sheep's, knives', everybody's, lass's, (or lass');

hers, countries', kids', firemen's, box's, somebody's, children's, thrushes', anybody's, deer's, heroes', its, James's (or James'), lives', boss's (or boss'), monkeys'.

10. WORKBOOK – *page 124*
KEY:

1. Mary's, Jane's; 2. Mary, Jane's; 3. Laurie's, Walt's; 4. Laurie, Walt's; 5. Jim, Joe's; 6. Polly's, Molly's; 7. Wake's, Wob's, Woo's; 8. Sam, Jane's; 9. Dr. Sow's, Dr. Pig's; 10. Tom, Suzy's; 11. Pat's, Mike's

2. hour's; 3. days'; 5. tomorrow's; 6. moment's; 7. dollar's; 10. years'; 11. tomorrow's.

11. WORKBOOK – *page 61*

a. This is the explanation and rule for the ie-ei spelling with examples and exceptions. The rule couplet at the top of the page should be memorized; it is expanded in sections on the page.

AA

b. The mnemonic sentences can be memorized to give mastery of the words.

12. WORKBOOK – *page 62*

AA

a. The most common exceptions which use <u>ei</u> instead of <u>ie</u> are included in the mnemonic sentence at the center top. It should be memorized.

b. KEY:

1st: priest, sleigh, brief, chief, veil, wield, cashier, ceiling, thief, yield, niece, grief, conceit, weigh, friend;

2nd: deceit, feign, pier, believe, piece, perceive, tier, reindeer, diesel, fiend, deign, grieve, reprieve, reign, relief;

3rd: field, series, siege, belief, freight, vein, shield, deceive, retrieve, neigh, receive, relieve, shriek, weigh, fierce.

APPENDIX

Angling Phonetic Skills Survey

This survey test ascertains the degree of a student's skill in using phonetic principles by the reading of unfamiliar nonsense syllables and words. It may be used at the beginning of training with *Angling for Words* to give indications of previous learnings and of areas for needed concentration. It can also be used at the end of each level or end of training as post-tests.

Instructions for its use, including a key for the teacher, precede the survey itself in this Appendix.

Sample Lesson Plan

This page is included as a suggested form to indicate the scope of the full *Angling* language training program; it emphasizes the inclusion of both reading and related spelling drills in the daily lessons. All items listed would not be applicable for each lesson. Such a sheet could be photocopied for the teacher's daily use, or the plan adapted according to teacher preference.

Reading Trophy Chart

This chart can be copied and used as a motivational device by which students can chart their progress in learning and applying the reading cards. The card letters or concepts are filled into the squares as they are learned, beginning at the bottom left. When completely filled in with the upward progress, the student has a fishing trophy.

KEY: From the <u>bottom</u> up:

<u>1st tier</u> at bottom – Level I

ĭ; t; p; n; s; ă; l; d; f; h; g; ng; ŏ; m; r; ĕ; y^c; y^v; ŭ;

k; nk; c^k; c^s; ck; b; j; ō; ed; ed^t; ed^d; w; wa; v; z; x; x^{gz}, qu; qua.

<u>2nd tier</u> – Level II and III

1st row: a-e; e-e; i-e; o-e; u-e; y-e; v-e suf.

2nd row: er; ur; ir; or; or^{er}; wor; ar; ar^{er}.

<u>3rd tier</u> – Level III

g^j; dge, sh; ch; ch^k; ch^{sh}; tch; th; ~~th~~; wh; ph; es.

<u>4th tier</u> – Level IV

V′/CV; VC′/V; V/CV′; VC/CV.

<u>Fish tier</u> – Levels V and VI

1st row: ee; ea$^{\bar{e}}$; ea$^{\breve{e}}$; ea$^{\bar{a}}$; o͞o; o͝o; ai; ay; oa; oe; ou; ou$^{o͞o}$; ow; ow$^{\bar{o}}$; au.

2nd row: aw; oi; oy; ue; ue$^{o͞o}$; ie$^{\bar{e}}$; ie$^{\breve{i}}$; ei$^{\bar{e}}$; ei$^{\bar{a}}$; ey; eu; ew; ui; ey$^{\bar{a}}$; -ous.

3rd: Level VI

o$^{\breve{u}}$; al; eigh; igh; kind-old; ble; V/V; tion; sion; sion^{zh}; silent; ear; ture; i^y;

ti; ci.

Evaluation Tests

Suggested reading and spelling tests are given for each level and can be used as pre-tests and/or post-tests.

For ease in administering, type the reading tests on index cards for student use. Spelling tests can be dictated from the manual.

Percentages or standards for each test given in the behavioral objectives for each level are only suggested and are arbitrary. Teachers can develop personal standards through local experience, remembering that errors do reveal continuing weakness.

The Angling Phonetic Skills Survey

Permission is given to reproduce this survey test.

To prepare for use of the survey:

1. Make copies of the two sheets for teacher's use in recording, one survey for each student to be individually tested. The same sheet may be used for a student's pre-test and post-test by marking with ink of two colors.

2. Prepare a set of unruled index cards for student test use, typing each non-sense word in the center of a 3x5 card in lower-case letters. The Level and number of each word can be written at lower right to facilitate keeping in order.

To administer the survey:

1. The student places the stack of cards, words up in the given order, before him and reads each nonsense word slowly and distinctly, emphasizing the final letters which are often "swallowed." Each card is turned over after being read, forming a stack of face-down cards above the unread stack.

2. For students frightened by unknown words, explain that each *could* be a real word and is often a syllable of a real word (as u<u>nit</u>, e<u>las</u>tic.) Ask him to try each word, even if he does not think he can read it correctly, since his response aids you in helping him by revealing the types of mistakes he makes.

3. If the student pronounces the word correctly, place a check on the line *before* the number. If there is an error, write the phonetic spelling of the *error* on the space corresponding to the location of the consonant, vowel, etc. mistake. (Headings KEY: C-consonant, V-vowel, CD-consonant digraph, VD-vowel digraph.)

4. It is advisable to place the survey sheet on a book, etc., tilted away from the student so that he is not watching the marking.

5. Sections for Level I-C, IV-B, and VI are spaced to show the two syllables and reveal division errors as well as others.

6. Errors on the test will clearly show which sections, letters, positions, or concepts need special or prolonged attention as work progresses through *Angling* and which can be covered more rapidly. For a student with good phonetic skills, it will reveal any specific weakness, which can then be corrected with practice for that Level in *Angling*.

KEY to Survey, using *similar real* words:

I-A
1. u<u>nit</u>
2. gas
3. step
4. <u>hom</u>iny
5. gut
6. rinse
7. sip
8. kelp
9. yam, lag
10. just, buzz
11. hot
12. cab, tax
13. quit
14. west

I-B
1. drop
2. <u>gl</u>itter
3. brad
4. smut
5. <u>c</u>risp
6. leg
7. <u>j</u>angle
8. list
9. p<u>lunk</u>
10. stomp

I-C
1. wig/lit
2. brad/doll
3. mess/met
4. spud/sip
5. hill/ban

II
1. bike
2. babe
3. meet
4. imm<u>une</u>
5. type
6. loaf

III-A
1. store
2. car
3. stir, fur
4. stir
5. blur
6. word

III-B
1. shun
2. chap, bag
3. whip
4. thad
5. fob

III-B
6. badge
7. much
8. peck, keg

III-C
1. cop
2. jet or (g)
3. pig
4. set
5. sill
6. <u>g</u>ondola
7. cat, lag
8. jig or (g)

IV-A
1. bow (no)
2. knee
3. day
4. "Y"
5. few
6. by

IV-B
1st choice
1. say´/bell
2. my´/pan
3. quo´/ta
4. fee´/dumb
5. pew´/lit

V
1. sleet
2. bean
3. spoof
4. gape
5. <u>za</u>´ny
6. toad
7. foul
8. powder
   or mow
9. dawn
10. draw
11. coil
12. boy
13. few
14. steal
15. cue

VI
1. fa´mous
2. bald
3. say
4. die
5. scrabble
6. joke
7. nation
8. fusion

Angling Phonetic Skills Survey

Name_____ Grade_____ Date_____

Level I - A

		C	V	C
____	1. nit	____	____	____
____	2. las	____	____	____
____	3. fep	____	____	____
____	4. hom	____	____	____
____	5. gud	____	____	____
____	6. ryn	____	____	____
____	7. sib	____	____	____
____	8. kel	____	____	____
____	9. yag	____	____	____
____	10. juz	____	____	____
____	11. vot	____	____	____
____	12. cax	____	____	____
____	13. quid	____	____	____
____	14. wef	____	____	____

Level I - B

		CC	V	CC
____	1. dron	____	____	____
____	2. glit	____	____	____
____	3. trad	____	____	____
____	4. smup	____	____	____
____	5. cris	____	____	____
____	6. bleg	____	____	____
____	7. jang	____	____	____
____	8. rist	____	____	____
____	9. lunk	____	____	____
____	10. fomp	____	____	____

Level I - C

		VC	CV
____	1. pliglit	____	____
____	2. bradnol	____	____
____	3. esmet	____	____
____	4. grudsip	____	____
____	5. hilban	____	____

Level II

		V	- con -	e
____	1. vike	____	____	____
____	2. habe	____	____	____
____	3. dete	____	____	____
____	4. bune	____	____	____
____	5. sype	____	____	____
____	6. rofe	____	____	____

Level III - A

		CC	V r
____	1. glor	____	____
____	2. clar	____	____
____	3. stur	____	____
____	4. smir	____	____
____	5. pler	____	____
____	6. wort	____	____

Level III - B

		CD	V	CD
____	1. shum	____	____	____
____	2. chag	____	____	____
____	3. whid	____	____	____
____	4. thap	____	____	____
____	5. phob	____	____	____
____	6. ladge	____	____	____
____	7. rutch	____	____	____
____	8. keck	____	____	____

Level III - C (c - g)

		C	V	C
____	1. cos	____	____	____
____	2. gep	____	____	____
____	3. lig	____	____	____
____	4. cet	____	____	____
____	5. cyl	____	____	____
____	6. gon	____	____	____
____	7. cag	____	____	____
____	8. gid	____	____	____

Angling Phonetic Skills Survey

Name_____Grade_____Date_____

Level IV - <u>A</u>

		C	V
____	1. bo´	_____	_____
____	2. ne´	_____	_____
____	3. da´	_____	_____
____	4. wy´	_____	_____
____	5. fu´	_____	_____
____	6. ki´	_____	_____

Level IV - <u>B</u>

		CV	CVC
____	1. savel	_____	_____
____	2. nipan	_____	_____
____	3. mota	_____	_____
____	4. redom	_____	_____
____	5. pulit	_____	_____

Level V

		C	VD	C
____	1. leet	____	_____	____
____	2. vean	____	_____	____
____	3. boof	____	_____	____
____	4. gaip	____	_____	____
____	5. zay	____	_____	____
____	6. noad	____	_____	____
____	7. roul	____	_____	____
____	8. pow	____	_____	____
____	9. taun	____	_____	____
____	10. daw	____	_____	____
____	11. coip	____	_____	____
____	12. hoy	____	_____	____
____	13. mue	____	_____	____
____	14. biel	____	_____	____
____	15. kew	____	_____	____

Level II

		C	V
____	1. ramous	____	_____
____	2. tald	____	_____
____	3. seigh	____	_____
____	4. digh	____	_____
____	5. habble	____	_____
____	6. jodle	____	_____
____	7. gration	____	_____
____	8. nusion	____	_____

NOTES:

Angling for Words
DAILY LESSON PLANS

Date_____   Student_____

  I. READING

    1. Reading Phono-Card responses

    Review – *Angling* pp. & col. _____

    _____

    2. Add card: _____

    Drill pp. & col: _____

 II. SPELLING

    1. Spelling Phono-Card responses

    Weak_____

    Practice_____

    2. Dictation: Teacher's Line, p. _____ or:

      1.   6.

      2.   7.

      3.   8.

      4.   9.

      5.   10.

    Phrases and sentences:

    3. Add card, response, or concept _____

    Practice_____

    4. *Angling Workbook* p. _____

 III. Handwriting emphasis_____

 IV. Other language activities _____

   _____

  V. Supplemental materials:

    Reading _____

    Spelling _____

NOTES:

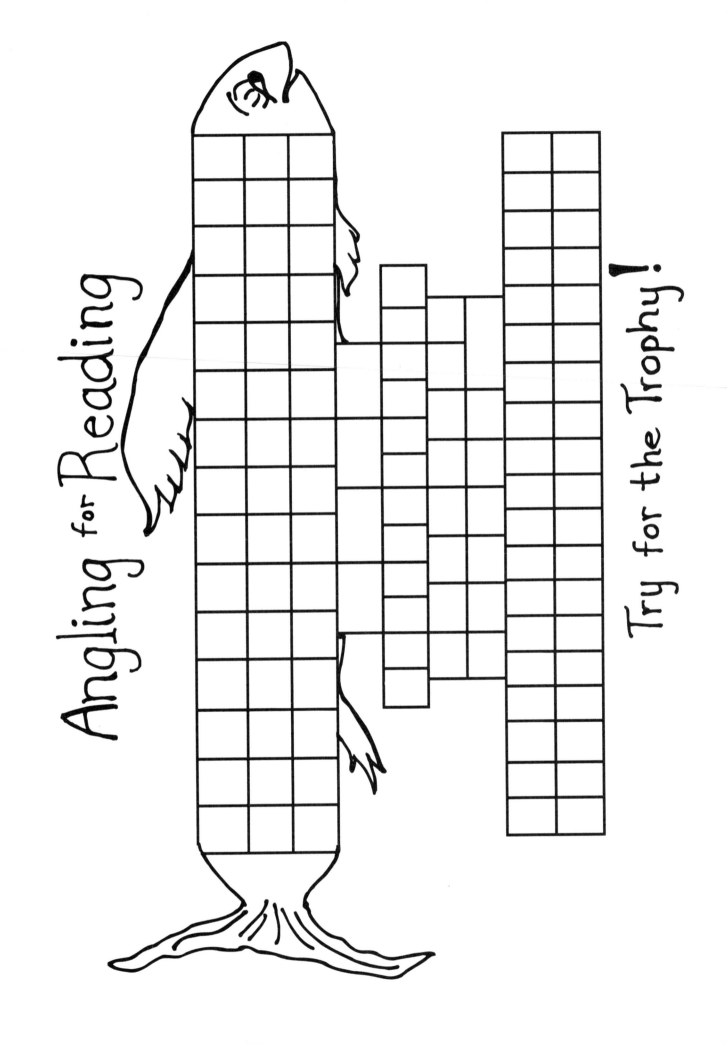

Angling for Reading

Try for the Trophy!

EVALUATION TESTS

Level I – *Reading*

Test I-A

is	hag	sled	yell
pit	singing	felt	spry
tin	doff	gallon	folly
spit	maps	arrest	graspstomp
flap	drop	empress	stomp

Test I-B Nonsense

ips	gop
feg	pless
moll	snad
han	gling
nift	strem

Test I-C

glut	junk	invent	fittingly
speck	exit	squib	tactlessness
blab	zigzag	quilt	manfully
flex	pygmy	quantum	barracks
wisp	wallet	prognostic	assembly

Test I-D Nonsense

kelk
lact
juff
nospo
guift

Test I-E Phrases

1. ringing bell
2. grand film
3. zestful dusting
4. pink felt pennant
5. waxy jonquil bulbs

Test I-F Sentences

1. Is a gremlin an elf?
2. Can possums do handsprings and fly?
3. Kim is gasping in Tom's hot tracks.
4. Ted tested himself constantly on kicking and passing
5. Conduct a census of ants in the sand!

Test I-G

cancel	ced
cyst	cosp
mascot	scim
cult	luncy
cinder	cang

Test I-H

mended	longed
backed	stumped
skinned	sanded
lifted	checked
napped	twisted

Level I – *Spelling Dictation*

Test I-1

is	yet
post	sly
miff	pesty
lass	magnet
rip	prong

Test I-2 Nonsense

frab	flet
pell	maff
lod	slon
disp	glig

Test I-3

jest	husky
mull	lax
skim	zestless
contact	wick
quilt	velvet

Test I-3 Nonsense

flug
brock
kess
vag
quing

Test I-4

1. a blast of wind
2. an empty basket
3. twin camps
4. rocky hills
5. scrub the deck

Level II – *Reading*

Test II-A

rap	fare	wince	taps
cope	mere	rarely	types
mete	tick	hopeless	muteness
cot	rake	capful	entire
pike	spices	tubless	mistakes

Test II-B Nonsense

deb	dyte
fide	num
hofe	zene
flimsate	gare
slon	crobeless

Level II – *Spelling Dictation*

Test II-I

hape	mute
van	lock
tire	stale
poke	quit
spare	quite

Test II-2 Nonsense

peb	fute
nafe	lig
jole	glom
rike	crad

Level III – *Reading*

Test III-A

pert	hurl	candor	dormancy
blunder	berry	spark	mortar
fonder	flirt	tartrate	interval
norm	enforce	parry	

Test III-B

gossip	gems	glint	merge
grant	gulf	gym	nudge
gender	gander	brag	dreg
stage	gist	lunge	barge
engage	ignite	dodge	ledge

Test III-C

shake	hitch
crush	blotch
harsh	shrine
churn	torch
drench	catchup

Test III-D

thick	those
throne	bathe
broth	welt
while	whack
phase	camphor

Test III-E

glasses	plates
mixes	ledges
lunches	rages
meshes	rates
tenses	traces

Level III – *Spelling Dictation*

Test III-1

butler
faster
storm
export
worst
spark
garner
carpenter

Test III-2

cage
goblet
abject
damage
hinge
gent
bridge
jobs
barge
hedge

Test III-3 (TT)

lunch
pitch
chap
march
chill
stretch
catch
bench

Test III-4

while
wither
farther
whips
bother
thank
whisper
taxes
wishes
bunches

Level IV – *Reading*

Test IV-A V′/CV

lotus
vacant
julep
bicorn
equal
tyrant
femur
omen

Test IV-B VC′/V

savage
critic
tepid
novel
static
peril
logic
baron

Test IV-C (Mixed)

comet
unit
dilate
glamor
cherish
halo
gyrate
epic

Test IV-D (TT)

depend	plasma
confident	adorn
provoke	lapel
diplomat	method
unite	ether
component	hydrant
culminate	phase

LEVEL IV – *SPELLING DICTATION*

Test IV-1

holy	bother	fiber	refresh
stupid	crater	rotund	migrate

Level V – *Reading*

Test V-A

creep	scoop
glee	tweezer
cheater	goober
entreat	behoove
repeal	shook
steady	grail
contain	await
dismay	curtain

Test V-B

gloat
loafer
reproach
doe
cloud
pounce
devour
youth
clown
chowder
bellow
aglow

Test V-C

sauce
assault
auditor
squaw
withdraw
void
sirloin
rejoice
convoy
disloyal

Test V-D

pursue	barley
brief	feudal
wiener	brew
calorie	pewter
tried	suit
seize	joyous
protein	mucous
vein	spied

Level V – *Spelling Dictation*

free	ouch
speed	brow
decay	fault
glow	thaw
subdue	moist
stoop	broiler
crook	convoy
scout	

Level VI – *Reading*

Test VI-A

pall
falter
neigh
thigh
stroll
rind
volt
mange
hover
baste

Test VI-B

hobble
stifle
haggle
ladle
canticle
resemble
participle
brickle
embezzle
ankle

Test VI-C

liable
peony
manual
folio
diagnose
radium
mania
conspicuous
oasis
alien

Test VI-D

portion
ration
contrition
exertion
devotion
ostentation
distribution
retardation
depression
occasion

Test VI-E

abundant
decency
dignitary
refinery
majority
poetic
wring
knelt
jamb
moisten

Test VI-F

doctrine
marine
preface
posture
bunion
gardenia
spacious
glacier
ambitious
initiate

Level VI – *Spelling Dictation* (TT)

Test VI-1

marble	soluble
coddle	freckle
bugle	sparkle
maple	cuticle

Test VI-2

ambition	caption
dictation	precaution
conviction	conversion
potion	erosion

Level VII – *Reading* (TT)

Test VII-A

rambled
ladled
noodles
bugler
sloping
spotting
slatted
glary
sparring

Test VII-B

rallied
pried
qualifies
sleepiest
envying
prayed
employed
spiciest

Level VII – *Spelling Dictation*

Test VII-1 (AA)

planing
later
slimy
lonely
coping
tuneful
duly
tameness
singeing
sliceable

Test VII-2 (TT)

dimmer
snappy
dusty
rapped
thinly
cooler
biggest
bigness
needful
landing

Test VII-3 (AA)

praying
prying
spied
funnier
joyful
relayed
defied
omitted
prohibited
regretting

Test VII-4 (TT)

clashes
paths
foxes
necks
thrills
delays
forties
convoys
armies
cavities

Test VII-5 (TT)

gulfs
shelves
fifes
wives
vetoes
heroes
gentlemen
mice

Test VII-6 (AA)

relieve
perceive
frontier
veil
shield
deceit
pierce
freight

Test VII-7 Student is to write the *possessive* form of the dictated words: (AA)

a boy	(boy's)
the elves	(elves')
some dogs	(dogs')
some men	(men's)
some ponies	(ponies')
a hero	(hero's)
a car	(car's)
five sheep	(sheep's)
his	(his)
nobody	(nobody's)

FOOTNOTES

[1] Emerald Dechant, *Diagnosis and Remediation of Reading Disability* (West Nyack, NY: Parker Publishing Company, 1968), pp. 189-90.

[2] Anna Gillingham and Bessie W. Stillman, *Remedial Training for Children with Specific Disability in Reading, Spelling, and Penmanship* (Cambridge, MA: Educators Publishing Service, Inc., 1956).

[3] Beth W. Slingerland, *A Multi-sensory Approach to Language Arts* (Cambridge: Educators Publishing Service, Inc., 1969).

[4] Aylett R. Cox, *Structures and Techniques . . . Remedial Language Training* (Cambridge: Educators Publishing Service, Inc., 1969).

[5] Georgie F. Green, et. al., *Alphabetic Phonics* (Cambridge: Educators Publishing Service, Inc., 1971).

[6] Cox, *op. cit.*

[7] Roger E. Saunders, "Dyslexia: More than Reading Retardation," *Dyslexia in Special Education* (Pomfret, CT: The Orton Society, 1965), pp. 26-9.

[8] H.R. Myklebust, *Auditory Disorders in Children* (New York: Grune & Stratton, 1954).

[9] Alfred Korzybski, in *Language in Thought and Action,* S.I. Hayakawa (New York: Harcourt-Brace, 1939), p. 179.

[10] H.R. Myklebust, *The Psychology of Deafness* (New York: Grune & Stratton, 1960).

[11] Sally B. Childs and Ralph deS. Childs, *Sound Phonics* (Cambridge: Educators Publishing Service, Inc., 1962), pp. 105-6.

[12] *Ibid.*

[13] Doris Johnson and Helmer R. Myklebust, *Learning Disabilities* (New York: Grune and Stratton, 1967), p. 239.

[14] Charles Fries, *Linguistics and Reading* (New York: Holt, Rinehart and Winston, Inc., 1963), pp. 139-45.

[15]Emerald V. Dechant, *Improving the Teaching of Reading,* Second Edition (Englewood Cliffs: Prentice-Hall, Inc., 1964), pp. 209-10.

[16]Aylett R. Cox, *Situation Reading* (Cambridge: Educators Publishing Service, Inc., 1972), p. iii.

[17]Paul Robert Hanna, *Phoneme-Grapheme Correspondences as Clues to Spelling Improvement* (Washington: U.S. Dept. of Health, Education and Welfare, Office of Education, 1966).

[18]Cox, *op. cit.*

[19]Aylett R. Cox, *Situation Spelling* (Cambridge: Educators Publishing Service, Inc., 1971).

[20]Childs, *op. cit.,* pp. 29-30.

[21]*Ibid.,* pp. 100-2.

[22]Dechant, *Improving the Teaching of Reading,* p. 222.

[23]Margaret B. Rawson, "The Structure of English: The Language To Be Learned," Reprint No. 35 (Towson, MD: The Orton Society, 1970), pp. 104-5.

[24]*Ibid.,* pp. 105-6.

[25]*Ibid.,* p. 108.

[26]*Ibid.,* p. 106.

[27]Lucius Waites, MD and Aylett R. Cox, *Developmental Language Disability . . . Basic Training . . . Remedial Language Training* (Cambridge: Educators Publishing Service, Inc., 1969), p. 2.

[28]*Ibid.,* p. 22.

[29]Marian T. Giles, *Individual Learning Disabilities Classroom Screening Instrument – Adolescent Level* (Evergreen, CO: Learning Pathways, Inc., 1973).

[30]Beth H. Slingerland, *Screening Tests for Identifying Children with Specific Language Disabilities* (Cambridge: Educators Publishing Service, Inc., 1973).

[31]Neva Malcomesius, *Specific Language Disability Test,* (Cambridge: Educators Publishing Service, Inc., 1967).

[32]Marian Monroe, *Children Who Cannot Read* (Chicago: University of Chicago Press, 1932), pp. 184-5.

[33]Margaret LaPray and Ramon Ross, "The Graded Word List: Quick Gauge of Reading Ability," *Journal of Reading,* 12:305-7, January, 1969.

[34]Elena Boder, MD, "Developmental Dyslexia: A Diagnostic Screening Procedure Based on Three Characteristic Patterns in Reading and Spelling," *Learning Disorders,* Vol. IV, ed. Barbara Bateman (Seattle: Special Child Publications, 1971), pp. 298-342.

[35]Monroe, *op. cit.,* p. 189.

BIBLIOGRAPHY

Boder, Elena, MD, "Developmental Dyslexia: A Diagnostic Screening Procedure Based on Three Characteristic Patterns in Reading and Spelling," *Learning Disorders,* Vol. IV, Barbara Bateman, editor. Seattle: Special Child Publications, 1971.

Childs, Sally B. and Ralph deS. Childs. *Sound Phonics.* Cambridge: Educators Publishing Service, Inc., 1962.

Cox, Aylett R. *Situation Reading.* Cambridge: Educators Publishing Service, Inc. 1972.

_____. *Situation Spelling.* Cambridge: Educators Publishing Service, Inc. 1971.

_____. *Structures and Techniques . . . Remedial Language Training.* Cambridge: Educators Publishing Service, Inc., 1969.

Dechant, Emerald. *Diagnosis and Remediation of Reading Disability.* West Nyack, NY: Parker Publishing Company, 1968.

_____. *Improving the Teaching of Reading,* Second Edition. Englewood Cliffs: Prentice-Hall, Inc., 1964.

Fries, Charles. *Linguistics and Reading.* New York: Holt, Rinehart and Winston, Inc., 1963.

Giles, Marian T. *Individual Learning Disabilities Classroom Screening Instrument –* Adolescent Level. Evergreen, CO: Learning Pathways, Inc., 1973.

Gillingham, Anna and Bessie W. Stillman. *Remedial Training for Children with Specific Disability in Reading, Spelling, and Penmanship.* Cambridge: Educators Publishing Service, Inc., 1956.

Green, Georgie F. et al. *Alphabetic Phonics.* Cambridge: Educators Publishing Service, Inc., 1971.

Hanna, Paul Robert. *Phoneme-Grapheme Correspondences as Cues to Spelling*

Improvement. Washington, DC: United States Department of Health, Education and Welfare, Office of Education, 1966.

Johnson, Doris and Helmer R. Myklebust. *Learning Disabilities.* New York: Grune and Stratton, 1967.

Korzybski, Alfred. In *Language in Thought and Action,* S.I. Hayakawa. New York; Harcourt-Brace, 1939.

Kottmeyer, William. *Decoding and Meaning.* New York: McGraw-Hill Book Company, 1974.

LaPray, Margaret and Ramon Ross. "The Graded Word List: Quick Gage of Reading Ability," *Journal of Reading,* 12:305-7, January 1969.

Malcomesius, Neva. *Specific Language Disability Test.* Cambridge: Educators Publishing Service, Inc., 1967.

Monroe, Marian. *Children Who Cannot Read.* Chicago: University of Chicago Press, 1932.

Myklebust, Helmer R. *Auditory Disorders in Children.* New York: Grune and Stratton, 1954.

_____. *The Psychology of Deafness.* New York: Grune and Stratton, 1960.

Rawson, Margaret B. "The Structure of English: The Language to Be Learned," Reprint No. 35. Towson, Maryland: The Orton Society, 1970.

Saunders, Roger E. "Dyslexia: More than Reading Retardation," *Dyslexia in Special Education.* Pomfret, CT: The Orton Society, 1965.

Slingerland, Beth W. *A Multi-sensory Approach to Language Arts.* Cambridge: Educators Publishing Service, Inc., 1969.

_____. *Screening Tests for Identifying Children with Specific Language Disabilities.* Cambridge: Educators Publishing Service, Inc., 1973.

Waites, Lucius, MD and Aylett R. Cox. *Developmental Language Disability . . . Basic Training . . . Remedial Language Training.* Cambridge: Educators Publishing Service, Inc., 1969.